P9-CLP-388

WRITING IS MY BUSINESS

THE STORY OF

O. HENRY

WRITING IS MY BUSINESS

THE STORY OF

O. HENRY

Peggy Caravantes

MORGAN REYNOLDS PUBLISHING

Greensboro, North Carolina

WORLD WRITERS

Charles Dickens
Jane Austen
Ralph Ellison
Stephen King
Robert Frost
O. Henry
Roald Dahl
Jonathan Swift

WRITING IS MY BUSINESS: THE STORY OF O. HENRY

Library of Congress Cataloging-in-Publication Data

Caravantes, Peggy, 1935-
  Writing is my business : the story of O. Henry / Peggy Caravantes.
— 1st ed.
      p. cm.
  Includes bibliographical references and index.
  ISBN-13: 978-1-59935-031-8 (lib. bdg.)
  ISBN-10: 1-59935-031-9 (lib. bdg.)
  1. Henry, O., 1862-1910—Juvenile literature. 2. Authors,
American—19th century—Biography—Juvenile literature. I. Title.
  PS2649.P5Z638 2006
  813'.52—dc22
  [B]
                                    2006016126

Printed in the United States of America
First Edition

*To my daughter-in-law Susan
and my son-in-law Bill—
Thanks for making my children happy.*

Contents

ONE
BOYHOOD
IN THE SOUTH

William Porter began to use the pen name "O. Henry" while he was in prison in the Ohio State Penitentiary. During his incarceration Porter began to write and sell stories to support his daughter. He needed a pseudonym because he did not want publishers to know he was a convict.

A number of different stories suggest how Porter chose the alias. Some say it was because Orrin Henry was the name of a guard at the prison where Porter served three years for embezzling bank funds. Others claim the name was an abbreviated version of the prison's name itself, the *Ohio State Penitentiary*. Yet another explanation has to do with a cat taken in by the Harrells, a family Porter lived with as a young man. He and the two Harrell sons found the little

Opposite: *O. Henry (William Sydney Porter).* (Courtesy of the North Wind Picture Archive.)

flea-infested black-and-white stray along the edge of the creek. They tried for months to become friends with the cat, but it only became wilder. Will Porter would put food on a stone in the middle of the creek and hide in the bushes. Eventually, the cat would creep out onto the rock and gulp down the food, ready to dart away at the first sound.

Will sometimes dangled cooked pork sausage and liver to try to get it to come closer. He would place the meat on the end of a fishing pole, ready to reel it in when the cat took a bite, but nothing could tempt the cat to come near humans. Sometimes when Will's friend Lollie went with him to the creek to watch the cat, they discussed all sorts of possible names for the little animal. Will finally decided to call the cat "Henry the Proud."

Will, determined to capture the cat, hit on a new plan— he would hypnotize it and then get it to come out of hiding. One day as the cat peeked from the bushes about ten feet away, Porter stooped down and looked the cat right in the eye. As he called softly, "Oh, Henry," the cat walked straight to him and rubbed against his leg. From that day on, everyone called the cat "O. Henry."

It is fitting that an amusing, probably embellished story would suggest the origin of O. Henry's name. So much of O. Henry's early life, like his fiction, is filled with whimsical anecdotes and colorful twists. Years later, when O. Henry was making his living as a writer in New York, he said, "I never met a man but what I could learn something from him. He's had some experiences that I have not had. He sees the world from his own viewpoint. If you got at it the right way,

Will Porter's hometown of Greensboro was a railroad hub for goods supporting the growing textile industry that surrounded the town. (Library of Congress)

you could extract something of value from him." He was, by nature and experience, a storyteller.

William Sidney Porter was born into a community on the outskirts of Greensboro, North Carolina, on September 11, 1862. Greensboro was a quiet town with a population of about 2,500. The Porters lived in an unpainted one-story house with three front doors and two rough granite slabs for steps. The house had been partly constructed from oak logs taken from the old Guilford Courthouse, near the area where Revolutionary General Nathanael Greene had fought General Lord Cornwallis and the British in 1781. The Battle of Guilford Court House had helped to turn the tide of the war in the Americans' favor.

Although the Porters were not wealthy, they boasted

good family connections. Will's maternal grandmother, Abia Shirley, had married the editor of the *Greensboro Patriot*, and his paternal grandmother, Ruth Coffyn Worth, was the sister of Jonathan Worth, who served as North Carolina's governor from 1865 to 1868.

Will's mother, Mary Virginia Jane Porter, had graduated from both Edgeworth Female Seminary and Greensboro Female College. At the age of twenty-five, she married one of the county's most eligible bachelors, Dr. Algernon Sidney Porter. Porter, like many doctors of the time, had learned medicine by working in a drugstore rather than by attending medical school.

By the time Will was born, Dr. Porter was considered the county's best physician. The onset of the Civil War increased Dr. Porter's workload dramatically. The Edgeworth Seminary was converted into a military hospital for wounded soldiers from both sides, and Dr. Porter tended the wounded soldiers as well as his own patients. Long after his death, Dr. Porter was remembered as "the best loved physician in Greensboro . . . kind to everybody, to children as well as to grown people."

Unfortunately, being a good doctor did not ensure a large income. Doctors seldom sent bills to their patients, who often did not have money on hand. There was an unwritten understanding that patients would settle their accounts when they sold their crops, but this did not always happen.

As an adult, Will did not remember his mother. She died from tuberculosis on September 26, 1865, at the age of

Will's father, Dr. Algernon Porter. (Courtesy of the Greensboro Historical Museum.)

thirty. Will was barely three. His only possession of hers was a bunch of yellowing poems tied with a faded blue ribbon. He was told that she liked to write and draw, just as he did. He would often stare at a daguerreotype, or early photograph, of his mother as a girl. He was told that he had inherited her talent for clever banter, as well as an artistic temperament and a shy personality. He later told a friend that he missed her all of his life.

Six months before she died, Will's mother gave birth to her third son, David Weir, who died only a few months later. Will could not recall his little brother but wondered if they would have become friends. He did not get along with his older brother, Shirley.

After his wife's death and the end of the Civil War, which forever changed life in the South, Dr. Porter withdrew from the world. He seldom talked to his sons, even when Will begged him to tell him more about his mother. Dr. Porter even gave up his medical practice and moved himself and his sons to live with his mother, the widowed Ruth Porter, who already managed a full house of boarders to earn enough money to support her large family.

Once, when Will saw his grandmother writing a stack of letters, he asked what she was doing. The old woman first took a puff of her clay pipe and then told him that she was sending notices to his father's patients who had still not paid their medical bills. Some of the bills were long overdue, and Mrs. Porter said the patients should pay what they owed. Her son could have been a rich man if he had collected even half of what was owed him.

Dr. Porter did little to help raise his sons. They spent most of their time with Grandmother Porter and Aunt Lina Porter. Sometimes Will wandered out to the barn to watch his father tinker with bits and pieces of machinery. Dr. Porter wanted to invent a perpetual motion water wheel as a means to make the family rich. Will, a shy, reticent boy, grew embarrassed about his unorthodox family situation around his friends.

Will and Shirley attended the one-room school located next door to their home. Aunt Lina ran the school. Miss Lina, as the students called her, became the closest thing to a parent Will and Shirley had. On Fridays during recess, Miss Lina, who based her instruction on good books, read aloud to her students. She would start an exciting story, read up to the climax, and then stop. That night she would open the school to anyone who wanted to hear the rest. As the eager students gathered around to hear the story's conclusion, Miss Lina gave the students popcorn and roasted chestnuts. She also encouraged original story telling. She

A sketch of Miss Lina's School as it looked when Will was a student. (Courtesy of the Greensboro Historical Museum.)

Will's aunt, Miss Lina, provided Will with his only formal education.
(Courtesy of the Greensboro Historical Museum.)

would start a story and then let each student add to it. Will's inventive additions were usually the most fascinating. Little did young Will know that storytelling would some-day be his livelihood.

Despite her excellence as a teacher, Miss Lina never did catch on to a trick Will pulled when she sent students to the chalkboard to work arithmetic problems. As they worked, she paced up and down the room to keep an eye on the students working at their desks. She held a switch for the swift punishment of any wrongdoer. Will was ambidextrous (able to write with both hands), and when he took his turn at the board he would start to do an arithmetic problem with chalk clasped in his right hand. Then, as Miss Lina turned around to walk toward the back of the room, he would grab another piece of chalk with his left hand and draw a left-handed caricature of Miss Lina. Of course, the other students burst into laughter. But Will was too quick for his aunt. He erased the drawing by the time she turned around.

Miss Lina took pride in Will, who always ranked at the top of his class. Although he excelled in arithmetic, geography, and grammar, history was his favorite subject. He was always fascinated by words, no matter how big and unfamiliar. He read the dictionary for fun. In later years, he remarked: "I did more reading between my thirteenth and nineteenth years than I have done in all the years since, and my taste was much better than it is now, for I used to read nothing but the classics."

Will did not fight or use vulgar language like his big brother, who was nicknamed "Shell." Shell, two years older than Will, had a taller frame, darker hair, and fewer freckles. Much rowdier than his shy brother, Shell did poorly in school and resented Will's good grades. Shell thought Miss Lina favored Will, and he took out his frustration on his younger brother. After Shell finished Miss Lina's school, he became a laborer, first on a farm and later in a construction camp. Will was glad when his brother left home, and the two were never close as adults.

From left to right: Shell Porter, Tom Tate, and Will Porter. (Courtesy of the Greensboro Historical Museum.)

Because his aunt's school was next door to their house, Will could not get away with playing hooky. Instead, he looked forward to weekends and holidays when he and his best friend Tom Tate roamed the fields and woods around Greensboro. Aunt Lina would pack them a lunch of jam sandwiches, slices of cold roast beef, hardboiled eggs and salt, and the boys would head off.

One of their favorite places to roam was an old Revolutionary War battlefield. Will read everything he could about the battle. He learned how the fighting became so furious that General Cornwallis ordered the artillery to turn and fire on a teeming mass of both British and American soldiers. The boys would scour the battlefield for remnants of the battle—buttons, flintlocks, bone fragments, a piece of shell, a sword blade. They searched the hardest for arrowheads left over from the days when Native Americans roamed the fields.

Will craved adventures and loved telling stories about his adventures even more. One of his most exciting tales was about the time he decided on a career as a whale catcher. He and one of his friends, J. D. Smith, decided to run away to the sea when they were twelve years old. The two boys used their savings to buy train tickets to Raleigh, North Carolina, and planned to walk from Raleigh to the coast. But when they reached Raleigh, they discovered that the coast was at least a month's walk away.

The boys were hungry, cold, and homesick, but they had no idea how to get back home. As they wandered down to the railroad tracks, Will and J. D. recognized a freight conductor from Greensboro who agreed to give them a ride back home if they would operate the brakes on the top of the train. The brakes were controlled by a wheel attached to a long rod that ran down to the wheel carriage. One toot meant to put the brakes on; two toots meant to take them off.

The ride home was terrifying. Crouched on top of the car, the boys clung to the railings as the train sped over the bumpy, curving track, tossing them from side to side. Will prayed as his teeth chattered in fright. When praying did not take his mind off the turbulent ride, he began to sing.

After he arrived back in Greensboro that night, Will crept home with his clothes covered in soot and cinders. He dreaded facing his family until he discovered that Aunt

Lina and his father did not even know he had run away. His brother Shell had told them Will was spending the day with a friend and would not be home for supper. Having his brother cover for him was a real surprise to Will; Shell did not help him out very often.

As much as Will enjoyed the unpredictable adventures with his friends, he also liked spending time alone. He often disappeared to a little hillside on Caldwell's Pond with a book and the pocket-size dictionary that his grandmother gave him for his ninth birthday. Most often the book he carried was a copy of *The Arabian Nights*, but he also read popular dime paperback novels such as *The Terror of Jamaica* or *The Wood Demon* by George Munro. Will followed the serial adventures of *Jack Harkaway* and *Dick Lightfoot* in an English magazine. The fantastic elements of these adventure stories would later find their way into his own fiction. Will identified with many of the characters in the exciting stories, but the clubs to which the fictional heroes belonged especially intrigued him.

Inspired by the stories he read, Will decided to organize the boys at school into opposing clubs, the Brickbats and the Union Jacks, and set up competitions between them. Will became leader of the Union Jacks, which also included Percy Gray, Tom Tate, and Jim Doak. The club members followed the rules of knighthood and bestowed titles on one another. The Union Jacks established their headquarters on the grounds of the burned-out Edgeworth Seminary, where they stored their weapons—wooden battle axes, shields, spears, sabers and saucepans used as tin helmets.

Ali Baba's son, who one day invited him to his father's house. On hearing that the new guest would eat no salt with his meat, Morgiana's suspicions were aroused, and she recognised him as the captain of the robbers. After dinner she undertook to perform a dance before the company, and at the end of it pointed a dagger at the captain, and then plunged it into his heart. Ali Baba was very much shocked, until Morgiana explained the reasons for her conduct; he then gave her to his son in marriage, and they lived in great prosperity and happiness ever after.

This illustration by Walter Crane is from an edition of The Arabian Nights *published in 1872 when Will was ten years old. It is easy to imagine why the colorful, exciting images would have caught his fancy.* (Courtesy of the Granger Collection.)

The Brickbats' headquarters were unknown to the Union Jacks, but Will and his club were determined to find it. The two groups often crossed paths but never actually clashed. Just as the two groups neared each other, "ghosts" would rise from the bushes right in front of the Union Jack army. Although Will did not believe in ghosts, he asked Shell about them just to be sure. His brother, who belonged to the Brickbats, assured him that ghosts did not exist, but he never told Will about the white sheet in the bottom drawer of his chest.

Will joined in the typical sports of his day. He excelled at roller skating. He liked to fence and often pretended that he was Sir Lancelot or Sir Galahad. Will also enjoyed mental exercise. Men often invited him to play chess with them because of his skill. He and Tom Tate sometimes spent entire afternoons taking long walks, reading, and talking. After their walks, they returned to the living room in Tom's comfortable house, where Will always felt secure because the Tates treated him like part of the family.

Another favorite game was "Indians." The boys would pull off their shirts and paint their bodies and faces with mud. Tom always struggled to get the mud all over Will's back to hide his many freckles. One morning, after raiding a large flock of turkeys that belonged to Tom's father, the boys placed their collection of tail feathers for war bonnets on the ground by the creek. They knew that Mr. Tate would not be pleased when he saw what the boys had done to his turkeys. But at that moment, they were more concerned about making bows and arrows for their weapons. When they later went hunting, using Mr. Tate's hogs for their prey, they accidentally shot an arrow into a prize hog. They chased the animal until they were exhausted, but they had to catch the hog in order to pull out the arrow before Mr. Tate discovered what happened.

As Will and Tom entered their teen years, Will developed his first crush on a girl, Sallie Coleman, who came each summer from Asheville to visit relatives in Greensboro. Too shy at first to speak to her, Will walked up and down in front of her house, looking the other way and whistling shrilly. Other times he showed off his roller-skating skills or walked on stilts to impress her. He wrote unsigned poems and put them in her mailbox, but Sallie knew who had written them.

However, Will had many rivals for Sallie Coleman's affection. One day several other boys left a bunch of magnolias on her front porch, and for days Sallie talked about the beauty and the sweet scent of the flowers. Will was determined to get Sallie the best magnolias he could find. Plenty of magnolias grew all around the town, and Will could have had any of them for the asking, but he wanted to do something romantic and daring. He knew that the most beautiful magnolias in Greensboro grew on the property of Judge Tourgée, who lived six miles outside town on Guilford College Road. Most of the town's young people considered the one-eyed, unpopular Judge Tourgée a tyrant, so even approaching his property was a risky act.

One midnight, Will and Tom hiked out to Judge Tourgée's home to gather magnolia blossoms for Sallie Coleman. With their heavy white blossoms weighting the branches, the magnolia trees stood in rows alongside the peach orchard. The flowers' sweet scent filled the air as Will whipped out his pocketknife and started to cut the stems. He handed the branches one-by-one to Tom, who laid them on the ground. Tom later told someone that he long remembered "the creepy sensation that I felt when we mounted the fence and started across the open field for the trees and the relief that came when we crossed that fence with the loot. We carried them back and laid them on Miss Sallie's doorstep." Young Will Porter was always up for a daring caper.

TWO
NEW EXPERIENCES

At fifteen, after he had finished Miss Lina's school, Will went to work in his Uncle Clarke Porter's drugstore. Will's family still suffered financial troubles, and so Will had to work.

Will served a five-year apprenticeship in the drugstore, which functioned as the gathering place for Greensboro's leading citizens. The men would come in to smoke cigars, drink whiskey, and discuss current events. Usually there was a chess game going on. Five-foot, six-inch Will was a thin, pale, but cheerful youth, popular with the customers. One of Will's friends said that Will "held a little court of his own at the drug store. He was the delight and pride of men two and three times his age." Many of them believed he would follow in the footsteps of his relative Thomas Worth, who had served on the art staff of Currier and Ives, well-known printmakers.

The amusing cartoons and caricatures Will drew made him a local celebrity. One time a man asked for credit when Uncle Clarke had left the drugstore for a few minutes. Will did not want to appear impolite by admitting he did not know the man's name, so he waited until the customer left and then drew a picture of him. When his uncle returned, he looked at the drawing and said, "Oh, that's Bill Jenkins out here at Reedy Fork. He owes me $7.25." Stories about

One of the many cartoons Will drew depicting daily life in his uncle's drug store. (Courtesy of the Greensboro Historical Museum.)

Will's artistic ability spread to other towns. Colonel Robert Bingham, the superintendent of the Bingham School in Mebane, North Carolina, heard about Will and offered him free tuition. Will declined because he had no money for books or clothes.

Working at his uncle's drugstore, Will learned enough to become a registered pharmacist with the North Carolina Pharmaceutical Association on August 30, 1881. Now his uncle, who liked to drink, could go home and leave his teenage nephew to keep the store open until midnight. Will occasionally pitched horseshoes behind his uncle's store or practiced pistol shots until he became an expert marksman. If he did get an evening off, he took his fiddle and joined some other boys in serenading college girls. But mostly Will stayed indoors, playing chess in the backroom when he had no customers in the store. Sometimes he played pranks, such as adding syrup to a urine specimen or displaying a snake in a jar of alcohol and claiming that it had been removed from a man's stomach. But the druggist's life began to take its toll. Will stayed inside too much and did not get regular exercise. He developed a hacking cough that concerned Dr. James Hall, a family friend.

In March 1882, Dr. Hall and his wife planned to visit their three sons who worked on a 250,000-acre guest ranch near Cotulla, Texas. A few days before he and his wife left, Dr. Hall told Will: "I want you to come with us, Will. You need the change, and ranch life will build you up." The doctor believed the dry air would help the young man's lungs. Dr. Hall worried the cough might signal the onset of tuberculosis, the disease that had killed Will's mother. Will, who had never left North Carolina, eagerly accepted the invitation.

In later years, what Will remembered most about Greensboro were the long hours he spent in the drugstore, the responsibility of his job as a pharmacist, and the shame he felt at his father not providing for his family. However, Will seldom discussed his feelings with anyone. His hidden emotions, coupled with the inability to face an uncomfortable situation, would plague him throughout his life.

The journey to Texas began by rail, which took Will and Dr. Hall's family to the guest ranch in La Salle County, Texas, where they changed trains for Houston. In Houston a friend of the Halls, Mr. Cave, came to the station to meet them. Mr. Cave, who was secretary and treasurer of the Houston and Texas Central Railroad, brought his daughter Lollie with him and introduced her to Will. Will almost broke Lollie's wrist with his enthusiastic handshake.

Lollie wore her long hair wrapped in braids around her head. Will said to her, "Why don't you wear your pigtails down your back instead of wrapped around your head? Don't you know it's bad for your brain to be heating it up all the time?" He continuously teased her as he waited for the next train. "What do girls like you do with their time—charm rattlesnakes, or chaps like me?"

Lollie called him Bill, and Will called her "Miss Lollie" or "Lolliepopy." When she asked him how he came up with that name for her, he said, "Oh, I don't know. I used to have frequent attacks of laryngitis. Sometimes my trachea has a fit, which enlarges my words and they come out effervescent." Will's train arrived and, with a merry twinkle in his eye, Will thanked Lollie for coming to meet him at the station. Lollie replied, "Southern girls, sir, are not in the habit of going to the station to meet boys." This began a friendship that lasted many years.

Dr. Hall's oldest son, Lee, a retired Texas Ranger captain, managed the ranch. Lee had started out as a schoolteacher, but soon moved into law enforcement, going from a city marshal's post to the legendary Texas Rangers. By the time Will met him, Lee Hall had acquired a national reputation for his ability to find and arrest desperadoes. After he married, Lee left the Rangers and took over managing the huge ranch empire owned by the Dull brothers of Harrisburg, Pennsylvania.

When Will arrived, Lee was in the midst of a fierce fight with fence-cutting thieves. Will thought Lee was a hero and later in his stories turned Lee into the model of the bold champion of law and order. Lee's three younger brothers—Richard, Frank, and Will—had all followed him to Texas to work on the ranch.

Richard Hall ran the sheep operation involving 60,000 sheep. When Dr. and Mrs. Hall ended their three-month visit and returned to Greensboro, Richard and his wife Betty invited Will to stay on with them and their young child. Will accepted the invitation, and the visit stretched to two years. The Halls lived in a remote, two-room cabin with one room divided by a curtain to serve as a kitchen

Although Texas had joined the United States as the twenty-eighth state in 1845, it was still largely a wild, frontier land in the 1880s when Will moved there and worked as a ranch hand. (Courtesy of the Granger Collection.)

and a dining room. Betty Hall and her daughter shared the other room as their bedroom. Richard, Will, and a hired hand all slept outside.

With its rugged outdoor activities, such as cattle roping and branding, Texas was a shock to the shy, artistic Will, but he flourished on the ranch. He was no longer the pale, underweight young man who had arrived only a few months earlier. His job herding sheep left him plenty of time to read, and the well-educated Betty Hall made her classic literature library available to him. As Will read, he kept his copy of *Webster's Unabridged Dictionary* close by.

Will took up learning Spanish and eventually became the best Spanish-speaking American on the ranch. He also picked up some German and French. But he did not stop at foreign languages. He learned to play a guitar, and his occasional duties filling in as a cook on the ranch helped him improve his culinary skills. He studied the names of Texas plants and trees, such as live oak, chaparral, mesquite, Spanish dagger, hackberry, and prickly pear.

Will also learned a few basic cowboy skills—lassoing cattle, dipping and shearing sheep, riding a horse. The local cowboys accepted Will into their group and eventually initiated him into their fraternity by pouncing on him one night as he lay curled up in his blanket on the ground. Six-shooters blazing, they dragged a saddle back and forth across his body. Once they were sure he was awake, they hazed him by thrashing him with a pair of leather leggings. After giggling at Will's howling for nearly an hour, the boys decided he had earned his spurs.

Once a week, Will left the ranch to ride his dun pony fourteen miles to pick up the mail at Fort Ewell. The four-hour ride to the combined store and post office was dull, hot, and dusty. One day Will met the niece of the store owner, M. P. Kerr. She was visiting from Brenham, Texas, for the summer and working in her uncle's store. Her name was Clarence Crozier and, although Will was immediately attracted to the brown-eyed sixteen year old, he was too shy to talk to her. They gradually became friends, and Will started to plan his trips to the post office so that he arrived at dinnertime, because he knew the family would extend an invitation for him to join their meal. However, he did not accept their offers. Instead, he would hang around until they finished their meal, when the family gathered to talk, play games, or sing along while Miss Crozier played the organ.

Will often stayed until ten o'clock in the evening. Sometimes, before heading back to the ranch, he and Miss Crozier would take a horseback ride, despite her aunt's objection. Mrs. Kerr did not want her niece to have anything to do with a poor ranch hand. When Miss Crozier ignored her aunt's advice not to see Will anymore, Mrs. Kerr resorted to bribery.

Miss Crozier had often remarked how much she would like to have Mrs. Kerr's large, white ostrich plume. Miss Crozier envisioned herself back in Brenham, impressing everyone with the white feather dipping down from her black velvet hat. Mrs. Kerr told her niece: "Forget that Porter boy, and the white plume is yours. Go back to your folks at Brenham. And when you get there think no more about him, and do not write."

Miss Crozier agreed not to see Will anymore and returned home without even saying goodbye. Her aunt never did give her the white feather, and Miss Crozier did not completely forget Will. After she died in 1935, a book collector paid a hundred dollars for a page from her yellowed autograph album with a love poem Will Porter had written on June 3, 1883.

Will was remarkably unfazed by her departure. He was accustomed to moving on when things did not work out.

"She has vamoosed," he wrote of Miss Crozier, "and my ideas on the subject are again growing dim."

Just as in Greensboro, news of Will's artistic talent spread. An Austin businessman, John Maddox, caught word of "a young fellow here who came from North Carolina . . . who can draw like blazes." When Maddox encouraged his friend Joe Dixon to write a memoir, to be called *Carbonate Days,* of his years as a gold and silver prospector in the Colorado Rockies, he recommended that Dixon check out the young man from North Carolina as a possible illustrator.

Dixon visited the ranch and liked what he saw of Will's sketches depicting life on the sheep ranch. He asked Will to prepare some illustrations for his book, and they worked together for the next three weeks. With forty illustrations carefully wrapped in a package with the manuscript, Dixon returned to Austin intending to get the book published. However, when he reread what he had written, he doubted the book's quality. He later revealed: "I hesitated no longer. I opened the package, and deliberately tore the story into fragments, chapter by chapter. Then I threw it into the placid waters of the Colorado River." When John Maddox learned what Dixon had done, he organized a search party that fished the manuscript out of the river. Even so, the manuscript was ruined.

Living with the Richard Hall family, Will became accustomed to depending on others to take care of him. In later years, Betty Hall recalled the youth who had stayed with them for two years as one who showed "no sense of responsibility or obligation or gratitude . . . and had never expressed any gratitude or repaid them [the Halls] for money." Nevertheless, the Halls felt protective toward Will and arranged for him to stay with another family in Austin when they decided to move to a ranch near Florence, Texas, in 1884.

Will traveled with them as far as Austin, a city that boasted more than 10,000 inhabitants. The University of Texas at Austin had just opened to its first class of students, and construction had begun on the new red granite state capitol with its glittering copper-plated roof.

The Halls made arrangements for Will to stay with the

Anglo-American settlers began arriving in Austin in 1835, when Texas was still part of Mexico. The town later became the capital of the Republic of Texas, then of the state. The capitol building, pictured below on the hill, burned to the ground several times during the mid-1800s. (Courtesy of the Granger Collection.)

Joseph Harrell family, who were also natives of Greensboro. The Harrells, who already had four sons—Harvey,
Dave, Joe, and Clarence—allowed Will to live as a non-
paying guest at their home on Lavaca Street. They treated
Will like a fifth son, and he stayed with them for three years.
Mr. Harrell and his sons enjoyed testing Will's vocabulary
skills. They often played a game with Will, calling out the
hardest words they could find in his dictionary—words
such as *recrudescence, sacerdotalism, phylogenesis,* and
zoophytical. They fined Will a nickel for every word he
could not spell and define. He seldom had to pay, and the
Harrells enjoyed showing off his verbal skill to their
friends.

Now twenty-one, Will Porter still made little effort to
start a career. He clerked at a cigar store and at Morley Drug
Company after receiving glowing recommendations from
several outstanding citizens in Greensboro. But working
in a drugstore in Austin was just as tedious as it had been
in Greensboro, and within a couple of months he quit.
Mostly he sat around the Harrells' house reading, drawing
pictures, or playing the guitar. He apparently felt no guilt
about living off the Harrells' generosity, and they seemed
to have no problem with their non-paying guest. They even
offered to send him to New York to study art. Porter
declined, either from a lack of self-confidence or an unwill-
ingness to work that hard.

Porter also continued to focus on his interest in music.
His pleasant bass voice earned him a place with the Hill City
Quartette, along with Ernest Hillyer, Howard Long, and

R. H. Edmondson. A contemporary observer described Porter as "the littlest man in the crowd. . . . He was about five feet six inches tall, weighed about one hundred and thirty pounds, had coal black hair, grey eyes, and a long, carefully twisted moustache." Young ladies in Austin considered it a treat to be serenaded in the evenings by these four young men singing such popular tunes as "Wait 'Till the Clouds Roll By, Jennie" and "In the Evening by the Moonlight." After their serenades, the quartet enjoyed pecan cakes, candy, and lemonade served by their audience. Porter also sang in three church choirs and took part in various theater productions.

In Austin, Porter renewed his friendship with Lollie Cave, who, along with her sister Rosine, spent vacations with an aunt in Austin. The entire family accepted "Bill" into their circle. Porter was especially close to Lollie's grandmother, whom he called "Granny."

Granny wore her hair twisted at the back of her head with a white shell comb tucked into the twist. One day Porter decided he wanted to brush Granny's long, silky hair. Granny did not especially want Porter to brush her hair, but she had a hard time refusing the charming young man. As Porter took out all the pins and the tucking comb, down came her long hair. He did the brushing and combing part perfectly, not pulling Granny's hair. In fact, she became so comfortable that she almost fell asleep.

When Porter had finished, he pinned Granny's hair back up and ran outside to get a big pink althea blossom, whose stems and leaves are stiff as wire. To make matters worse, the heavy, cut blossoms ooze a thick, sticky fluid. Porter stuck the flowers into Granny's hair—ooze and all. To Granny's horror, black ants infested the blossoms. They crawled in Granny's ears and eyes and then down her back. Porter and Lollie picked ants out of Granny's tangled hair all night.

Porter pulled another prank one time while Lollie's aunt played the piano. While everyone danced, Granny's little black and tan rat terrier named Pompossy ran among the dancing feet. The dog liked Porter, who had taught it to sit on its hind legs and to balance a pecan on the end of its nose and then flip it into its mouth. During the dancing, Porter took the dog upstairs. When he returned, Will was wearing one of Granny's loose-fitting dresses with big puff sleeves and had tied a nightcap under his chin, turned up his pant legs, rolled down his socks, and wore a big blue sash around his waist. The dog, meanwhile, wore Lollie's best point lace handkerchief as a hat and a pink ribbon with a bow around its neck. Porter had fastened a lace corset-cover around the dog for a dress and tied several finger rings with pink ribbons to its tail, which stuck straight out. With the dog in his arms, Porter rejoined the dancers, circling the room with the dog as his new partner.

In any given situation, Will saw potential for humor and surprise, elements that would become trademarks of his short fiction. He joined a National Guard unit called the Texas Rifles and traveled with them to Fort Worth to guard a depot from potential damage from strikers. They had to travel through the town of Waco, where an Austin girl who had earlier caught Porter's eye was visiting. Porter wired and asked her to meet him at the depot. He perched himself on the cowcatcher, the iron grill on the front of the train that clears obstructions from the tracks, so he could surprise and wave to the young lady as the train pulled into the station.

Even after he left the city, people in Austin recalled stories of Porter's escapades. One of the favorites involved him and several other members of the Texas Rifles while they were at a military camp in Lampasas. The young men had permission to attend a big dance at the Park Hotel, but their passes expired at midnight. The guards were having such a good time they did not realize that twelve o'clock had come and gone, and the corporal of the guard marched into the hotel with a squad to escort the soldiers back to camp. Porter sent one of his friends to ask the guards to leave their guns at the door in order not to alarm the young ladies.

This seemed a sensible request to the guardsmen, who agreed to stack their rifles at the door. As they did so, Porter and his friends snuck out the back door and walked quietly around to the front, where they grabbed the guards' guns and took off toward camp. As Porter and his comrades walked back to camp, they pretended to be guardsmen escorting a prisoner. They even went so far as to form a circle around one of the men, who acted as their prisoner. As they approached the camp's gate, Porter confidently yelled out that they were bringing in a man under arrest and that everyone else should step aside. The trick worked. Porter and his friends marched inside and quickly scattered to their own tents. When the real guard squad returned with no arms and no prisoners, they were arrested as impostors and placed in the guardhouse overnight. Porter later revealed that "There was quite a time at the court-martial next morning, at which the corporal and his body were given extra duty for their inglorious behaviour on the previous night, but no one ever knew our connection with the story."

THREE
LIFE IN AUSTIN

Porter's social life in Austin eventually became so active that he was forced to find a regular job to pay for all his fun. In the fall of 1886 John Maddox, who had solicited Porter's help with the illustrations for Joe Dixon's book, offered him a job as a bookkeeper in the prestigious real estate firm of Maddox Brothers and Anderson. Porter earned a hundred dollars a month, a generous salary considering he had no experience as a bookkeeper. Maddox asked another member of the firm, Charles E. Anderson, to train Porter, who quickly caught on and worked for the firm for about a year. Anderson later said, "He learned bookkeeping from me, and I have never known any one to pick it up with such ease or rapidity. He was number one."

With a regular paycheck in hand, Porter blossomed. He bought some good clothes and took pride in his

Will Porter in his early thirties. (Greensboro Historical Museum)

appearance. He began to part his hair in the middle and comb it down in smooth wings over his broad forehead. He let his mustache grow long, waxing and twisting it in the style of Spanish caballeros.

The Texas Land Office in Austin, where Will Porter worked from 1887 to 1891.
(Library of Congress)

That same year, Porter's friend Richard Hall from the ranch at Cotulla was named Texas land commissioner. He helped Porter obtain a job as an assistant draftsman for cartography, or map drawing, in the Land Office. Porter quit his bookkeeping job. He enjoyed the fast pace of the office that dealt with problems settling new territory in the West, and he was fond of his new surroundings.

Porter joined the Austin Grays, one of the National Guard companies. This group, which regarded military service as more of a social activity than a serious commitment, attended a ceremony to lay the 18,000-pound granite cornerstone of the new state capitol. It was at this event that twenty-five-year-old Porter spotted his future bride. Athol Estes Roach had been chosen by her classmates at Austin High School to place their mementos in the cornerstone of the new capitol.

Athol was born in Clarksville, Tennessee and came to Austin with her widowed mother, who moved to the Texas capital with her new husband, the widower P. G. Roach.

Athol attended public school. Although her family would have preferred to send her to private school, they simply could not afford private school tuition. Athol was always popular. Classmates covered her desk with candy hearts, poems, flowers, and fruit in elementary school, and in high school she was an outstanding student. When seventeen-year-old Athol placed the souvenirs selected by her classmates into the cornerstone of the capitol, she added one of her own long, golden curls.

During the ceremony, Porter first noticed Athol because of the sheer, delicate, ruffled rose-pink dimity dress she wore. Her smile, charm, and long, shining golden hair caught his eye. That night he met her at a couples dance.

Porter was struck by Athol's beauty, and she later confided to a friend that she was crazy about him because he was so funny and clever. However, Athol's mother thought she was too young to see Porter. But this did not stop Porter. He had to find ways to see his sweetheart behind her mother's back.

Athol's friends came up with creative ways to help the couple meet throughout her senior year. Porter sent her notes and waited outside the school to carry her books.

Sometimes he helped her with her English homework. When she received an assignment to describe the entertainment given during a benefit of a local church, Porter suggested that Athol write: "The tableaux were all on a large scale, intricate, elaborate, and very elegant. Colored lights were burned, and the young ladies in their groupings and graceful draperies were very beautiful." Athol's English teacher must have wondered at Athol's enthusiastic description of the young ladies.

Athol's strict mother was not Porter's only problem. He soon learned that Lee Zimplemann, the son of a wealthy German family, was trying to win her over, and Zimplemann had Athol's mother's approval. He had even surprised Athol with a beautiful opal friendship ring and a bracelet with a lock as a pre-engagement token that only he had the key to open.

When Athol's graduation day arrived, she, along with the other thirteen members of her high school class, read her essay at the ceremonies. Athol titled the essay "Three Fold is the Pace of Time" and concluded it with a statement that seemed directed at Porter: "Look not back upon the past, it comes not again, improve the present, it is thine, and go forward to meet the shadowy future without fear and with a manly heart."

A few days later, Mrs. Roach asked Athol to go into town on a quick errand to pick up a spool of thread before the stores closed in the late afternoon. Just as she left the house, Athol tore her white dimity dress. Mrs. Roach scolded Athol and told her not to leave the house with a torn skirt but Athol insisted she needed to hurry to town before the store closed.

After she purchased the thread and left the store, Athol met Porter on the street. As soon as he approached her, Porter tried to persuade Athol to elope with him that night. Athol resisted at first. "I love you, Bill, and would marry you if it were not for Mother," she said. "I don't want to go against her advice, as I have never disobeyed her. She has funny ideas, but I am sure my love for you is strong enough to withstand any opposition. No matter what comes I will marry you—some time."

Porter refused to take no for an answer. "Not sometime—but now, Athol," he told her. "Honey, I am not marrying your mother, so if you think more of her than you do of me I guess I shall have to marry the policeman's daughter by his third wife. Maybe I have 'marry' on the brain but marry I must. I want someone to cook my corn-pone. I'm tired of boarding house hash. You think it over quick-like, if you don't want to prolong my vocabulary."

Will's smooth talk seemed to work, and Athol agreed to elope with Porter that evening. Porter asked her a second time if she would really go through with the elopement. She replied: "I'm going to be firm, firm as a rock!" Porter knew that he had to hurry because he had learned that his rival planned to come to Athol's house that evening to make the engagement formal.

The first thing Porter did was to cut Zimplemann's bracelet from Athol's wrist. Then, with the help of his close friends, Mr. and Mrs. Charley Anderson, Porter and Athol obtained an after-hours marriage license from the county clerk. Later in the evening they rented a carriage and rode west out of town to Dr. R. K. Smoot's home on what is now West Sixth Street in Austin. Dr. Smoot was the pastor of the Southern Presbyterian Church, where Athol and Porter sang in the church choir. The Andersons accompanied them as witnesses.

The Smoots were sitting on their front porch when they heard a team of horses on the old plank bridge that spanned Shoal Creek. A carriage in the neighborhood signaled an unusual event at that time of day. Mrs. Smoot said to her husband, "Papa, it must be a wedding." Charley Anderson got out of the carriage and walked up to the porch and told the Smoot family: "There's romance in the air. I've got a couple down at the gate that want to get married." After making arrangements for the wedding, Anderson went back to get his wife, Porter, and the bride.

As Athol got out of the carriage, she exclaimed, "Oh, Will, my dress is torn!" After her groom found a pin and hid the tear, he told Athol: "Marrying in a torn dress is quite distinctive—a lot better than a torn heart." Dr. Smoot recognized Porter and Athol as members of the church choir, but he hesitated to marry them without Mrs. Roach's permission. A nervous Porter told Dr. Smoot that the couple was determined to marry that night, and he threatened to find someone else if Dr. Smoot would not perform the ceremony. Recognizing they were both of age and could be wed elsewhere, the minister agreed. The Andersons, Mrs. Smoot, and fourteen-year-old Lawrence Smoot served as witnesses. Reverend Smoot performed the ceremony at 9:30 p.m., July 1, 1887.

The newly married couple went back to the Andersons' house, where they waited for Charley Anderson to break the news to Athol's parents. Mrs. Roach reacted hysterically at first. Charley Anderson finally convinced her that it was her duty to give the young couple her blessing. When the newlyweds arrived at her house, Mrs. Roach had finally calmed down enough to tell them, "God bless you, my children," but she held a grudge against Reverend Smoot for several months, refusing to speak to him or to attend church.

Porter and Athol lived in the Andersons' home for the first six months of their marriage. When Athol became pregnant, the couple moved to a cottage at 505 East 11th Street. Porter walked to work at the Land Office, where his job did not demand much effort. With Athol's encouragement, he began to write stories and sketches and to send his work to magazines. He sold his first story for six dollars to *Truth* and told some friends: "It will keep the chafing dish bubbling and buy steak and onions." However, it would be ten years before the publication of his first short story in a national magazine.

The young couple participated in Austin's social life. The next few years were some of the happiest in Porter's life, despite the loss of his first-born son, Anson. The baby died a few hours after birth on May 6, 1888. Athol was left so weak from the pregnancy and delivery that Porter and the Roaches feared she would die too. By then the Roaches had completely forgiven Porter and Athol for eloping and had become their strongest supporters. Mrs. Roach managed both households while Athol recovered.

Porter's hundred dollar monthly salary that had seemed so big when he was a single man was not enough for a family. He began to search for other ways to make money. One day as he looked through some maps in the Land Office, he found a piece of unclaimed land in Wilbarger County. He bought the property for fifty dollars and a few months later sold it for nine hundred. He could have continued buying up unclaimed properties and reselling them for a long time, but he discovered something else in the Land Office that convinced him he could make more money faster. On one old map, he noticed the marking for a lost gold mine and decided to try to find it. After unsuccessfully trying to enlist the help of his brother Shell, Porter hired a wagon and equipment and drove eighty miles to seek the mine himself. He found nothing.

When Athol became pregnant for the second time, the couple moved to a house on East Fourth Street next door to Athol's parents. On September 30, 1889, she gave birth to their second child, a girl they named Margaret Worth. Athol had a hard time recovering from Margaret's birth, and they moved in with Athol's parents for several months. Perhaps because of her difficult recovery, Athol became very possessive of Porter. If he came home a little late, she threw herself on the floor and screamed. When she was well enough to go out again, she enjoyed starting public arguments that humiliated her husband.

To raise Athol's spirits and to get her away from the hot Texas summer, Porter arranged for her, her mother, and baby Margaret to go for a visit to Nashville, Tennessee, and from there to Greensboro to see Aunt Lina. Lina's mother and Porter's grandmother, Ruth Worth Porter, had just died. Near the end of the summer, Porter joined them and enjoyed showing off his bride and new baby. However, his initial reaction upon returning to Greensboro was not happy:

> I got off at the old depot, and then commenced the strange feeling of loss, depression, and change that so much alteration wrought. I walked down the old

Porter himself took this photograph of North Elm Street, a main thoroughfare in his hometown of Greensboro, North Carolina. (Courtesy of the Greensboro Historical Museum.)

familiar streets and gazed in deepest wonder at the scenes around me. The streets seemed narrower, the houses smaller and meaner; every prospect had shrunken and grown into ruin and decadence. I met men in the street by whose side I had grown up from my earliest boyhood. They all passed me with either a curious stare or a careless glance.

The Porters went back to Texas. Aunt Lina promised to visit them soon. While they had been out of town, the election of a new governor in 1890 had ended Richard Hall's stint as land commissioner. Porter's position had been a political appointment, meaning he also lost his job to a supporter of the new governor. In February, Charles Anderson helped Porter land a job as a teller at Austin's First National Bank, which was owned by George W. Brackenridge and managed by his two brothers, John Thomas and Robert J. Brackenridge. Porter received the same hundred-dollar-a-month salary that he had at the Land Office.

Banking did not suit Porter, who found his many tasks to be dull. When customers came to his window, he took their deposits and cashed their checks and drafts. He was also responsible for keeping the books on his transactions. To offset the boredom, he drew sketches during slow periods. Despite his bookkeeping experience, he was soon having trouble with the accounts.

The Brackenridge brothers managed the bank very casually. They allowed customers to write checks even when there was no money in their accounts. The employees helped themselves to money whenever they needed it,

Porter in his cash cage during his employment at the First National Bank of Austin as a bank teller. (Courtesy of the Austin Public Library.)

The East Fourth Street house, where Athol and Porter lived in Austin, is now a museum dedicated to Porter's life. (Library of Congress)

sometimes putting an IOU in the cash drawer, sometimes not. Porter once spent days searching for missing money until a bank official walked by and said: "Porter, I took out $300 last week. See if I left a memo.; I meant to."

Porter looked for ways to increase his income and maybe get out of the bank. Athol encouraged him to write, and he submitted stories to national magazines and eastern newspapers. In the spring of 1893 they moved into a cottage at 308 East Fourth Street, across the street from the Roaches. The house had an extra bedroom to accommodate Aunt Lina's expected visit.

In the evenings the Porters sat on the narrow front porch with its scrolled railings. The five-room house had no gas or electricity; coal stoves heated the small home. The entire family slept in the same room, lit by kerosene lamps.

When the Chicago World's Fair opened in 1893, friends invited Athol to go with them. Porter secretly saved money to pay for Athol's trip. Just before her friends left for Chicago, Porter proudly presented her the money. Athol accepted the money with one of her sweet smiles. She had

Athol, Margaret, and Will Porter in 1895, while the family was living in Austin. (Courtesy of the Austin Public Library.)

decided not to go on the trip—but did not tell her husband. The next day she spent the money on things they both could enjoy. When Porter came home that night, new muslin curtains hung in the windows and new matting with a Japanese pattern covered the pine floors. A pair of wicker rockers sat side by side on the front porch.

Athol later told some friends, "I just couldn't go on a jaunt and leave Will here to work all summer and not have any fun. Now he'll have just as much fun out of the money as I do. You see I bought *two* rockers. I'm playing fair." Later, Athol's unselfishness became the basis for one of Porter's most famous stories, "The Gift of the Magi."

As the Porters' daughter, Margaret, grew older, her father delighted in his delicate, blue-eyed, fair-skinned child. He played games with her, drew funny pictures, and sang humorous songs. When the children in the neighborhood sent valentines to one another, Porter drew all of Margaret's cards. The Porters spent their summers at Richard Hall's large brick home in South Austin, which he let them use when he and his wife went back to their ranch. The house was near Barton Springs, a large swimming area fed by ice-cold springs. Margaret especially enjoyed the extra space to play outdoors, and her father said that he was glad for her chance "to know the joys of chasing chickens and getting redbugs on her legs."

By the late fall of 1894, money was regularly missing from the First National Bank. Some of it was the result of loose banking practices. But a federal bank examiner, F. B. Gray, discovered shortages in accounts Porter managed.

To this day no one knows for certain if Porter simply mismanaged his bookkeeping or whether he withdrew small sums with the intention of paying them back or just stole them. It is known that the bank's owners took responsibility for the shortages and did not want to prosecute him. In November Porter confided to his old friend Lollie Cave Wilson that he knew who was taking the money, but did not specify a name. He said the man was a good friend of his whom he trusted would straighten matters out if given time. No one can say whether Porter was telling the truth or not.

The owners eventually admitted to the bank's loose practices. J. M. Thornton, who had preceded Porter in the bookkeeping position, testified in court that there were discrepancies before Porter took over. Based on these two pieces of testimony, the grand jury decided it did not have enough evidence to charge Porter. That decision would have ended the issue if the federal bank examiner had not decided to pursue prosecution of the case. Gray believed he had compelling evidence of Porter's embezzlement on fifty different occasions. He quietly headed to Washington, D.C., to obtain an indictment.

In December 1894, after three years of accounting for other people's money and thinking that the accusations were behind him, Porter resigned from the bank. He wanted to devote his time to *The Iconoclast*, a weekly newspaper he had bought from W. C. Brann the previous March. Local real estate developer James P. Crane was Porter's partner. They wanted the paper to convey current events in a

humorous fashion, and to include short sketches, drawings, and poems.

Porter drew all the cartoons and wrote most of the copy.
He promised his readers "to fill its pages with matter that
will make a heart-rending appeal to every lover of good
literature, and every person who has a taste for reading
print; and a dollar and a half for a year's subscription." The
first issue came off the presses on April 28, 1894. Soon
afterward, Crane moved to Chicago, and Porter hired Dixie
Daniels, a printer, as his associate. The first two issues were
a success, selling all of the thousand copies printed. After
the first two issues, they changed the paper's name to *The
Rolling Stone* and published it weekly.

In what was to become a pattern for obtaining material
for his short stories, Porter spent hours in the local bars,
drinking heavily. Daniels, who often accompanied him,
later said, "We would wander through streets and alleys;
meeting with some of the worst specimens of down-and-
outers it has ever been my privilege to see at close range.
I've seen the most ragged specimen of bum hold up Porter,
who would always do anything he could for the man. His
one great failing was his inability to say 'no' to a man."

This tendency to give away his money, along with heavy
drinking, added to Porter's financial worries. He began
playing in poker games that often lasted into the early
morning hours. Not knowing where her husband was or
what he was doing, Athol became convinced he was having
an affair. Stories abounded about her midnight visits to
Porter's office, where she pounded on the locked doors,

A page from Porter's humorous weekly magazine, The Rolling Stone.
(Courtesy of the Austin Public Library.)

sure that a woman was in the room with him. Whether her fears were justified has not been verified, although several acquaintances suggested Athol was right to be suspicious. An unidentified woman did make a scene at the railroad station when Porter later left Austin.

FOUR
HARD TIMES

Porter often went to San Antonio to try to sell advertising for *The Rolling Stone*. There he rented a two-room house on South Presa Street, in a wild part of San Antonio. Porter loved the town's narrow, crooked streets. He liked to visit the Buckhorn Saloon, go to the theater, and talk to tamale vendors in "Little Mexico."

Hoping to sell subscriptions to his newspaper in San Antonio, Porter hired a co-editor, Henry Ryder-Taylor, an Englishman, to edit a San Antonio page for *The Rolling Stone*. But the newspaper's success did not last. When Porter drew a cartoon of a fat German professor leading an orchestra and beating the air wildly with a baton, it offended the large German community in Austin, and they canceled subscriptions and advertisements. Then Porter let Ryder-Taylor convince him the paper should become involved in a heated San Antonio mayoral race, which cost him San Antonio advertisers.

To keep *The Rolling Stone* going, Porter borrowed from family and friends. Money became such an obsession that he was again drawn to stories of buried treasure. He heard rumors of 20,000 gold pieces stolen during Santa Anna's march on Texas. An aged Mexican, who claimed to be a descendant of the man who buried the treasure, offered to sell a map to Porter and two of his friends. The man assured them the map would lead them to the buried treasure. Porter and his friends bought the map.

When they located matching tree markings near Shoal Creek in Austin, Porter and his friends believed they had found the exact spot of the buried treasure. One dark night, armed with a Colt pistol to protect their treasure, they dug about seven feet deep in the ground when suddenly they heard a horrible screeching and howling. They hid behind some trees and peeked out to see a screaming creature dancing in circles around the hole they had just dug. The three men rushed for their buggy, bumping into trees and bushes and one another. The next day they heard that a madman had escaped from a nearby asylum the previous night and had been picked up near where they were digging. Porter and his friends decided to give up on their attempt to find buried treasure. The experience later became the basis for the short story "Buried Treasure":

It was a wonderful June day.... I investigated the hill shaped like a pack-saddle from the base to summit. I found an absolute absence of signs relating to buried treasure. There was no pile of stones, no ancient blazes on the trees, none of the evidences of the three hundred thousand dollars, as set forth in the document of old man Rundle.

I came down the hill in the cool of the afternoon. Suddenly, out of the cedar-brake I stepped into a beautiful green valley where a tributary small stream ran into the Alamito River. And there I was startled to see what I took to be a wild man, with unkempt beard and ragged hair, pursuing a giant butterfly with brilliant wings. "Perhaps he is an escaped madman," I thought; and wondered how he had strayed so far from seats of education and learning.

After a few months, Porter realized that the newspaper was failing. He was offered a job in Washington, D.C., as the head of a humorous newspaper similar to *The Rolling Stone*. The Porters sold their furniture to prepare for the move, but then Athol became seriously ill. Doctors diagnosed her with the dreaded tuberculosis. Porter decided to stay with her and gave up the Washington job.

The last issue of *The Rolling Stone* came off the press on April 27, 1895, a year after it had started. Between that time and the following October, Porter and his family were completely dependent upon his in-laws. Two payments of five and ten dollars for short humorous sketches sent to a Cleveland newspaper were his only income in that six-month period.

There was an old fellow from Austin
Stopped over a day in Boston
And he sais: "This here town
covers most too much ground
It's just the right size to get lost in.

One of Porter's humorous sketches and an accompanying limerick. (New York World)

Porter moved to Houston in the fall of 1895, leaving his six-year-old daughter Margaret and his ill wife in Austin with Athol's parents. There he received an offer to work for the Houston *Post*. Colonel R. M. Johnston, the newspaper's editor, had been impressed with Porter's writing in *The Rolling Stone*. He invited Porter to come work for him as a general utility writer for fifteen dollars a week. It was not enough to support his family, but Porter accepted anyway. The job gave him something to do, and left open the possibility of a raise at some point. For the first time in his life, Porter would earn a regular, if meager, salary for writing.

At the Houston *Post*, Porter had various reporting duties, mostly covering society affairs, which he despised. A few months later Athol and Margaret joined him in Houston, where the family stayed in a boarding house on Caroline Street. Porter contacted his friend, Lollie Cave Wilson, who lived on a farm near the city. She invited them to visit the farm, which became a new playground for Margaret. Although the family once had a scary ride when a horse ran away with their buggy and almost turned them over, they enjoyed spending time on the ranch. They had no idea that the days in Houston were the last time they would live together as a family—the

By the time Will Porter moved to Houston in the mid-1890s, it was a growing city, with a population of 45,000. The discovery of oil there, in 1901, would quickly transform Houston into one of the most important urban centers of the United States. (Library of Congress)

investigation of the First National Bank was being re-opened upon direct orders of the comptroller of currency in Washington.

As Porter's assignments on the *Post* improved, he began to write a column, called "Some Postscripts," that included longer sketches that were popular with the paper's readers. Porter's salary rose to twenty dollars a week, then twenty-five, the top wage paid to any Houston *Post* journalist. During this time Porter wrote fifty-five sketches and short stories. These were not collected into a book until more than twenty years after his death, and some are still not available in printed form. He was still developing his own style.

This idyll ended when the bank examiners called Porter back to Austin in June 1896 to face five charges of embezzling money from the First National Bank. By the time he arrived in Austin, his father-in-law and a good friend had already posted his $2,000 bond. He was charged with embezzling a total of $5,487.02 over the course of several months.

Porter insisted he had never taken money for himself. Sometimes he had trouble balancing his accounts because of the loose practices at the bank, but he claimed he had never stolen money. Porter's father-in-law and some friends offered to make up the $5,000 deficit. However, bank examiner F. B. Gray insisted that Porter stand trial the next year. Porter returned to Houston on February 14 and sent Athol and Margaret back to Austin on June 20.

Although Porter had asked for an extension of the trial date so he could look at all the bank books for the years he worked there, he apparently never looked at the books and made no effort to prepare a defense. He did not even consult with his attorneys. He simply waited for the trial to begin in July. Because he did not talk about the situation, his friends at the *Post* assumed he was not worried.

On July 6, 1896, Porter boarded a train to return to Austin for the trial. In his pockets he carried $260 collected by friends at the Houston *Post* who believed in his innocence. Whether his subsequent decision to flee was a whim or a premeditated plan is another unanswered question about Porter's life. Many of his friends believed the former—that he panicked as the train rolled over the tracks, ashamed at the thought of going to prison and wondering if anyone would ever believe in his innocence.

Others believed that Athol, although she did not approve, knew about his plans all along. A close friend in Austin, the couple's next-door neighbor, said that Athol did know Porter planned to run. He said Athol had even given Porter her watch to sell to help with his expenses. Lollie Cave Wilson later revealed a conversation she had with Porter in late June: "When I met him he was perfectly calm and seemed anything but frightened. However, his expression was very serious and the old smile was gone. His first words were, 'Polly-O, the little black crow has alighted again, and again we fly away. . . . You won't agree with me— neither does Athol—but I am going away, maybe forever. . . . I will send for Athol and Margaret as soon as I am able.'"

Whatever the truth, when the train stopped in Hempstead, Texas, Porter stepped off and bought a ticket for New Orleans. There he started using his brother's name, Shirley

Worth. He took a job with a local paper. Casual acquaintances recalled him mingling with other journalists. No one knows how long Porter stayed in New Orleans, but it was probably only a little while. He must have used the time to wander extensively throughout New Orleans because many details from the city show up in his later stories. At some point he hopped a run-down freighter bound for Trujillo, Honduras. Apparently, he planned to stay out of the United States for three years, until the statute of limitations, the period of time he could be legally tried for the crime, ran out.

Little is known of Porter's activities in Honduras, a favorite hiding place for North American fugitives because it did not have an extradition treaty with the United States. In Central America, Porter met the notorious bank robber Al Jennings. They formed a friendship that continued throughout their lives. When the $30,000 taken from his most recent bank theft ran out, Jennings began to plan another robbery and invited Porter to join him and his brother Frank in the holdup. Porter declined, but Jennings liked Porter and wanted him to share in the loot, although the Jennings brothers really did not need his help. Finally, Jennings asked Porter if he could just hold the horses while the two brothers robbed a bank. Porter replied, "I don't believe I could even hold the horses."

While he was in Honduras, Porter wrote to Athol about once a month. To keep postal authorities from learning his whereabouts, Porter sent the letters to their next-door neighbor, Mrs. Louis Kreisle. He wrote about digging

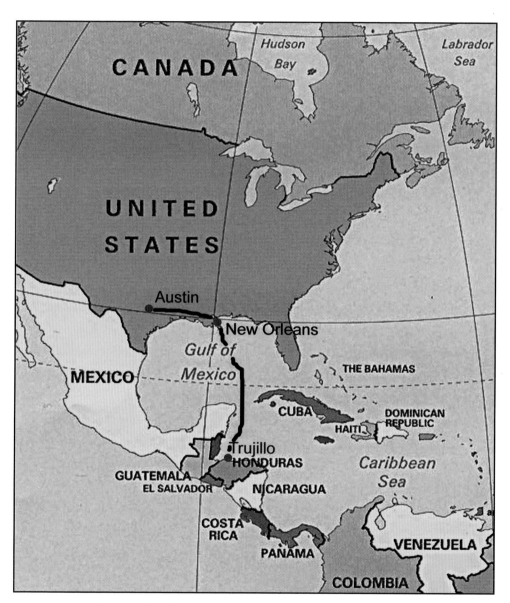

Porter first traveled from Austin, Texas, to New Orleans, Louisiana, before taking a ship to Trujillo, Honduras.

ditches and other manual labor and said he often had nothing to eat but bananas. This seems unlikely, since he had access to Al Jennings's loot. He continued to drink heavily while in Central America.

Porter wanted Athol and Margaret to join him in Honduras. He had found a school for Margaret. However, Athol was too ill to travel. She had tried to earn some money and had started a business course, but had to give it up. Despite her illness, Athol made a point lace handkerchief to raise money, and some of her friends raffled it for twenty-five dollars. She used the money to send Christmas presents to her husband. Porter did not learn until months later that his wife had a fever of 105 degrees on the day she packed his gifts.

A short time later his mother-in-law sent word that Athol was dying. Porter raised enough money to sail back to New Orleans, but not enough to get to Austin. From New Orleans he sent a telegram to his father-in-law on January 21, 1897: "Wire me twenty-five dollars without identification quick. Can't get my check cashed." Porter arrived in Austin on February 5, 1897, and turned himself in to face trial. He had stayed in Honduras less than a year.

Athol believed in Porter and encouraged him to defend himself against the charges. His return had a positive effect on her health and "she fairly radiated with joy at the thought [of Porter's returning of his own free will]. People surely would acknowledge his innocence." Instead of working to clear his name, Porter devoted his entire attention to his young wife. On Sunday mornings he carried her in his arms to a carriage. They drove to Dr. Smoot's Presbyterian

Church, where they sat outside beneath a window to listen to the sermon and the music.

The improvement in Athol's health brought about by her husband's return did not last. Then, in May, he received word that his Aunt Lina had died without ever having visited them. But Porter barely acknowledged his aunt's death as he worried about his beloved wife. Athol defended his innocence until the moment she died in her sleep on July 25, 1897, at the age of twenty-nine.

Athol's death devastated eight-year-old Margaret. To comfort her, Porter took her out for nightly drives into the countryside in their buggy until she fell asleep. Porter tried to be both father and mother. He played games with Margaret, drew funny pictures, told her stories, and sang humorous songs. He bathed, fed, and dressed her and read her Uncle Remus stories. When she went to bed, she gripped her father's thumb while he tapped out the rhythm of a melody on her wooden headboard to see if she could guess the tune. Once she fell asleep, Porter substituted a small toy for his thumb before he left the room.

Porter maintained a good relationship with his in-laws after his wife's death. They too believed in his innocence and proved to be his strongest supporters throughout the rest of his life.

Porter needed money. Both he and the Roaches faced financial hardships. He began writing again. On December 2, Porter sold his first short story, "The Miracle of Lava Canyon," to S. S. McClure Company of New York. The story was not published in the company's national magazine until five months later. In accepting the story, the editors wrote: "Your story, 'The Miracle of Lava Canyon,' is excellent. It has the combination of human interest with dramatic incident. If you have more like this, we should like to read them." The sale was about all the good news that Porter heard as he awaited trial. He avoided his friends and became so despondent that he temporarily considered suicide.

Prosecutors had postponed the trial until February 1898, due to Athol's illness and death. However, because of Porter's flight to Honduras, they had added two more charges. In an attempt to strengthen their case before the trial, prosecutors combined and dropped various indictments until the final amount for which he was tried amounted to only $854.08. When the trial began, Porter insisted on his innocence. But he was still grieving over the death of his wife and took no interest in the proceedings.

Over the years various biographers have claimed that the bank examiners were vindictive and made Porter a scapegoat. Some years later a prominent Austin banker revealed: "It might just as well have been me as Will Porter. I applied for that position in the First National Bank when Will Porter got it. He was older and had more experience, so they gave him the job. I thought he was fortunate and I was out of luck, but it was the other way around. Had I gotten the job, I would have been sent up. The Federal authorities were tired of that bank's methods and they had to make a killing. However, he just cinched things at Hempstead when he flew the coop." Others claimed that Porter had a poor defense.

The Travis County jail in Austin, Texas, where Porter was held before his transfer to the Ohio State Penitentiary. (Library of Congress)

The jury had delibrated for only an hour when it returned with a guilty verdict. They believed Porter had taken cash deposited by bank customers and tried to cover up the theft by not recording the transaction. They also had a hard time believing that an innocent man would have run away. Years after the trial, a member of the jury wrote: "The money was gone. The defendant offered nothing to show his innocence. When a ballot was taken, the jury was unanimous for a verdict of guilty."

Porter was given the lightest sentence the law allowed—five years, to be served at the Ohio State Penitentiary. While waiting two months in the Travis County jail for the trip to the federal prison, Porter spent his time writing. To obscure his identity, he changed the spelling of his middle name from "Sidney" to "Sydney" and dropped "William." Sydney Porter left for Ohio on the morning of April 22, 1898. Several friends stood at the railroad station to see him off. They later said that Porter looked more like a man about to start a trip than a prisoner bound for the penitentiary. Outwardly calm, he thanked and shook hands with many of his friends as he prepared to board the train.

After the conviction and sentencing, Mr. and Mrs. Roach promised to take care of Margaret and to keep her from learning that her father was in prison. Mr. Roach even sold his grocery store in Austin and moved the family to Pittsburgh to lessen the chances of Margaret's hearing gossip about her father. In a rare comment about the accusations against him, Porter later wrote to his mother-in-law: "I am absolutely innocent of wrong-doing in the bank matter, except so far as foolishly keeping a position that I could not successfully fill."

FIVE
PRISON AND REDEMPTION

Porter entered the Ohio State Penitentiary on April 25, 1898, the day the Spanish-American War began, as prisoner #30664. At the age of thirty-six, his hair was already streaked with gray. He listed newspaper writer as his primary occupation, and pharmacist as a second occupation to prison authorities. This last skill served him well in prison, and his knowledge of medicines, plus his model behavior, led to his appointment as the night druggist in the prison hospital.

Even in prison, Porter found someone to watch out for him. The prison physician, Dr. John M. Thomas, apparently believed Porter when he said: "I never stole a thing in my life. I was sent here for embezzling bank funds, not one cent of which I ever took. Someone else got it all."

Working in the prison hospital, Porter fared much better

The Ohio State Penitentiary in Columbus, Ohio, where Will Porter served his jail term from 1898 through 1901. (Library of Congress)

than the average inmate. In fact, he was treated more like an employee than a prisoner. He slept on a cot in the hospital rather than in a cell and walked freely around the prison grounds. His helpfulness, sense of humor, and quiet dignity made him a favorite with both jailers and fellow prisoners.

However, the sensitive Porter viewed the penitentiary with sheer horror. In letters to his mother-in-law, he wrote: "I never imagined human life was held as cheap as it is here. The men are regarded as animals without soul or feeling." Sickness, death, and suicide were common. Prisoners who could not, or would not, work were beaten or sprayed with heavy jets of water aimed at their faces. When other prisoners learned of Porter's writing ability, they urged him to write about the prison atrocities, but he ignored their requests. He insisted it was not his responsibility to remedy "the diseased soul of society. I will forget that I ever breathed behind these walls."

After he completed his work in the hospital each night, Porter settled down about midnight to write stories. When they were finished, he sent them to New Orleans, where the sister of a fellow inmate mailed the stories to magazines. That was so that editors did not know he was a convict. "Whistling Dick's Christmas Stocking," the first story to show his pen name O. Henry, appeared in *McClure's* magazine in 1899.

Porter wrote fourteen stories while in prison. Editors rejected only two of them. The stories showed the full range of his abilities and his development as a writer. Not one of them dealt with his trial and imprisonment, but many of his later stories can be traced to his prison experience and to tales recited to him by other inmates. Many of them deal with redemption. One of the most famous is "A Retrieved Reformation," in which a famous safecracker, Jimmy Valentine, changes his lifestyle when he falls in love with a banker's daughter.

While in jail, Porter wrote his daughter, Margaret, a letter every Sunday. He kept up the pretense of being a traveling writer. "I am busy all the time writing for the papers and magazines all over the country, so I don't have a chance to come home, but I'm sure going to try to come this winter," he wrote in one. He sent Margaret's letters in covering envelopes addressed to various postmasters. The postmaster removed the letter addressed to Margaret and then sent it to her with that city's postmark. This helped Porter maintain his appearance of a busy businessman who traveled widely.

In his deepest despair, Margaret was his only incentive to not give up. His letters show how much he loved her, and how much he wanted her to be happy.

> July 8, 1898
> MY DEAR MARGARET:
> . . . I am so sorry I couldn't come to tell you good-bye when I left Austin. You know I would have done so if I could have. . . .
> I think about you every day and wonder what you are doing. Well, I will see you again before very long.
> Your loving
> PAPA

Porter wanted Margaret to enjoy herself, and in the same July 8 letter, he wrote: "I'm so glad you and Munny [Margaret's name for her grandmother] are going to Nashville. . . . Now you must have just the finest time you can with Anna and the boys and tumble around in the woods and go fishing and have lots of fun. . . . So you be just as happy as you can, and it won't be long till we'll be reading Uncle Remus again of nights."

Porter worried about Margaret's health because of the history of tuberculosis on both sides of the family.

Porter's first letter to Margaret from prison, May 8, 1898. (Courtesy of the Greensboro Historical Museum.)

May 17, 1900
DEAR MARGARET:
It has been so long since I heard from you that I'm getting real anxious to know what is the matter. Whenever you don't answer my letters I am afraid you are sick, so please write right away when you get this. . . .

After serving some time as prison drug clerk, Porter was made the bookkeeper to the prison steward. The steward's office was in a separate two-story building that held general shops with all kinds of provisions. Porter could come and go from it as he wished. Whenever he received money for selling a story, he selected little gifts from the shops to send to Margaret. One time, when she had not written to him for some time, he sent her a watch. Then he wrote: "I hope your watch runs all right. When you write again be sure and look at it and tell me what time it is, so I won't have to get up and look at the clock." From time to time, he sent her money: "twenty nickels to spend for anything you want."

Margaret also received letters from her father about going to school and the importance of learning:

October 1, 1900
DEAR MARGARET:
. . . I suppose you have started to school again some time ago. I hope you like to go, and don't have to study too hard. When one grows up, a thing they never regret is that they went to school long enough to learn all they could. It makes everything easier for

them, and if they like books and study they can always content and amuse themselves that way even if other people are cross and tiresome, and the world doesn't go to suit them.

No copies of Margaret's letters survive, but Porter's letters often refer to what she had written: "I'd have liked to see the two fish you caught. Guess they were most as long as your little finger, weren't they?" Another time when Margaret got too close to a horse, he wrote, "I was . . . very, very sorry to learn of your getting your finger so badly hurt. I don't think you were to blame at all, as you couldn't know just how that villainous old 'hoss' was going to bite. I do hope that it will heal up nicely and leave your finger strong."

The days when Porter received letters from Margaret were special, but she could never write enough letters to satisfy him.

> MY DEAR MARGARET:
> . . . I haven't had a letter from you in a long time.
> . . . You don't want to go to work and forget your old Pop just because you don't see much of him just now, for he'll come in mighty handy some day to read Uncle Remus to you again and make kites that a cyclone wouldn't raise off the ground. So write soon.

To get her to write more often, Porter even tried a little bribery: "Now, if you will write me a nice letter real soon I will promise to answer it the same day and put another dollar in it." Margaret and her father found holidays difficult, but Porter still drew Valentine's, Easter, and Christmas cards for Margaret to give to her friends. He looked forward to his reunion with his daughter and wrote about plans for the future in most of his letters: "I am learning to play the mandolin, and we must get you a guitar, and we will learn a lot of duets together when I come home."

Porter's cleverly disguised letters coupled with Margaret's grandparents' measures to hide her from the truth succeeded in keeping her from learning about her father's imprisonment. Not until 1913, when she was an adult, did Margaret learn that her father had served time in jail. One biographer angered Margaret when he stated that she had learned about her father's imprisonment during her childhood. She wrote in the margin of the first-edition copy of the biography: "NO! He *never* told me. I found out only after his death!"

Will Porter entered prison a defeated man. He had lost his wife, his job, and his freedom. Dr. Thomas, the prison physician, said, "I have never known a man who was so deeply humiliated by his prison experience." Because of his good behavior, Porter gained more than five hundred days of early release time and left the prison on July 24, 1901. He had not seen his daughter, now twelve years old, for three years and three months.

Before he left the prison, jailers issued Porter the standard cotton suit, worth about four dollars and fifty cents. He always liked to dress well and hated the cheap suit. He asked Al Jennings, his friend from Honduras who was

Porter's friend, the notorious outlaw Al Jennings, was eventually released from prison, where he was serving a life sentence, on technicalities in 1902. He received a presidential pardon in 1907, went on to become a gubernatorial candidate in Oklahoma in 1914, but lost. (Courtesy of the Granger Collection.)

now a fellow inmate and secretary to the warden, to see if he could get back the tweed suit Porter had worn when he entered the prison, but another departing convict had already taken it. However, a prison official let Jennings select a piece of fine brown wool fabric, and the prison tailors made Porter a new suit to wear when he left the Ohio Penitentiary.

The prison also gave him a pair of squeaky shoes, a railroad ticket, and five dollars. He also had about sixty dollars earned from the sale of a short story. Porter used hair tonic to take the squeak out of the shoes. His friends at the prison knew how much he liked to dress up. They took up a collection and bought him a pair of yellow gloves he wore for years. For the rest of his life, he always kept at least one pair of yellow gloves on hand.

The world that Porter faced upon his release was vastly different from three years earlier. Realism was the new vogue in fiction. Writers increasingly concerned them-selves with the plight of the "little man" and those who lived at the bottom of society. The Socialist Party in the United States, which advocated limits on personal wealth and fought to improve the lives of workers and the poor, was gaining popularity. In September 1901 President William McKinley would be assassinated and the new president, Theodore Roosevelt, would usher in a new era in domestic politics that began to rein in some of the power of giant corporations.

After his release, Porter headed for Pittsburgh, Pennsyl-vania, where Margaret lived with his in-laws at the Iron Front Hotel, which was located in the toughest part of the city. He hated seeing his daughter in such shabby surround-ings. But he had been gone so long that he was a virtual stranger to his daughter, who hardly recognized him at first. He had gained weight in prison. Becoming reacquainted with his almost teenaged daughter was harder than he had expected.

Porter stayed in Pittsburgh for almost a year, but he disliked the city. He worked at a newspaper, the *Dispatch*. At the same time, he wrote short stories at a furious pace, publishing more than twenty-five in 1902 alone. Between the two jobs, he earned about $150 a month.

Porter lived in constant fear that another ex-convict would recognize him and say, "Hello, Bill; when did you get out of the O.P. [Ohio Penitentiary]?" He struggled over keeping "O. Henry" as a pen name and tried other pseudonyms: Olivier Henry (chosen when a publisher insisted on a name instead of the letter O), James L. Bliss, and S. H. Peters. At one time, he had three short stories running in the same magazine, all under different aliases.

By early 1902 Porter knew that he needed to get to New York if he wanted to succeed as a writer, but he did not have enough money to go to the city. He wrote to Gilman Hall and Richard Duffy, editors at *Ainslee's Magazine,* who had accepted seven of the last eight short stories he submitted to them. He asked the men to send him one hundred dollars against future earnings so that he could travel to New York. He claimed to need the money because his business had gone broke. They sent him the hundred dollars.

As he prepared for his trip, he bought some new clothes, and a friend gave him a dollar to buy two more pairs of yellow gloves. He knew that he needed to provide for Margaret's care as well as start to repay the $10,000 already spent by Mr. Roach in caring for her. Before he knew it the hundred dollars were gone. He wrote a second letter begging for another hundred. Before sending any more money,

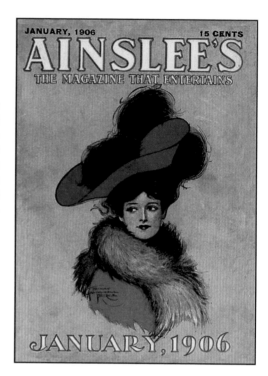

JANUARY, 1906   15 CENTS

AINSLEE'S

THE MAGAZINE THAT ENTERTAINS

JANUARY, 1906

Founded in 1898, Ainslee's started out as a general interest magazine, but adopted an all-story policy in the fall of 1902. In addition to O. Henry, Ainslee's *published the work of writers such as Jack London and Stephen Crane, as well as many others.* (Library of Congress)

however, Gilman Hall decided to have a graphologist, or handwriting expert, examine Porter's handwriting to reveal his character traits. The handwriting expert stated that Porter was a good risk—trustworthy, honest, and straightforward.

By the time Mr. Hall decided to take a chance on giving Porter the second hundred dollars, Porter had almost given up hope of getting the money. When the check arrived, he knew that it was his last chance to get to New York. He had to go, even at the risk of being recognized. Only one person in New York, his old friend and prison mate Al Jennings, knew him as Will Porter. Before leaving Pittsburgh, Porter wrote to Jennings: "By the way, please keep my nom de plume strictly to yourself. I don't want anyone to know just yet."

Porter's willingness to go to the big city, where he knew no one and had no guaranteed job, indicates how much confidence he had developed in his writing ability. A shy man, he would not have gone to New York if he did not believe he could succeed. Upon arrival, O. Henry went to the offices of *Ainslee's Magazine* to meet Gilman Hall and Richard Duffy. He wore new clothes— a gray suit with a brightly colored tie and a high-crowned black derby. He did not talk much at the first meeting. He feared that if he said too much he might reveal his past. When they went out to eat in a restaurant, he behaved rather strangely, darting glances from side to side. Hall soon suspected O. Henry might have a past: "I thought that he had perhaps killed some one in a ranch fight, for he had told me that he had lived on a ranch in Texas. This inference was strengthened by finding that he was a crack shot with a pistol." Gilman Hall did not learn about the prison record until after O. Henry's death, but over the years no one in New York came to know O. Henry better or to have a deeper affection for him.

By July, O. Henry had settled in New York and was regularly selling stories to magazines. The stories mostly concerned the lives of Americans who, for one reason or another, had fled to Central America. Using the mythical Republic of Anchuria and its port city Coralio as the setting, O. Henry poured out story after story about the lives of these expatriates. The timing was perfect. President Theodore Roosevelt was planning the Panama Canal project, which made Central America newsworthy. O. Henry produced four stories using this setting between 1902 and 1903.

After O. Henry had been in New York for some time, the city began to intrigue him. He was an unlikely candidate to become New York's most popular storyteller. He had no ambition to capture the spirit of the city. His only aim was to make money. He explained: "Writing is my business; it is my way of getting money to pay room rent, to buy food and clothes and Pilsener [a light beer]. I write for no other reason or purpose." He had little formal education and a deep desire to keep others from learning the details of his personal history. He had never lived in a big city and had not personally known anyone in the book publishing business before his arrival in New York.

However, he began to see the city with fresh eyes and grew to love how it attracted immigrants from all over the world. He came to see it almost as a sort of fantasy city, a setting for a modern version of *The Arabian Nights*. He referred to New York as "Baghdad on the Subway" and to himself as the Caliph of Baghdad. He roamed the streets alone after dark, absorbing the feel and pulse of the city. He once said, "When I first came to New York, I spent a great deal of time knocking around the streets. I did things then that I wouldn't think of doing now. I used to walk at all hours of the day and night along the river fronts, through Hell's Kitchen, down the Bowery, dropping into all manner of places, and talking with any one who would hold converse

O. Henry's primary New York stomping grounds surrounded Madison Square, where he could wander and observe the interactions of many different walks of life. (Library of Congress)

with me." He took his story ideas from the people. He tried to simply tell their stories as they would if they could write like he could, and in the process he revealed the city's strengths and weaknesses.

He told stories about the prostitutes, many of whom left the sordid conditions in sweatshops to take up life on the streets. Others had been kidnapped off the street and placed in prostitution, a life from which they could never escape. He wrote about street gangs so large that they resembled small armies. But, despite what he revealed about life on the underside of New York, he never saw himself as a writer with a message. He was an entertainer, not a reformer. In prison he had refused to write letters to the authorities about the horrible jail conditions, and as a chronicler of his adopted city he refused to take an editorial stand against the poverty, crime, and violence his stories depicted. When it came to fiction, he was a storyteller, not a journalist.

O. Henry wrote his picturesque sketches of New York City in a small room that he rented at the Marty, a French hotel near Madison Square. He could have afforded a nicer place to live. His income from seventeen stories in 1902 was about $1,200, enough to provide a pleasant lifestyle. A four-course meal at his favorite restaurant, for example, cost thirty-five cents and a suit of clothes, ten dollars. He paid a dollar a day for his room. But his chronic drinking always kept him short of money.

SIX

DEMAND FOR STORIES

As O. Henry's popularity grew, so did the demand for new stories from the editors of popular magazines that sold for ten or fifteen cents a copy. Many of these stories came to be known as his "Southern stories," because they reflected O. Henry's memories of his childhood in North Carolina. Despite his former eagerness to leave his time in Greensboro behind, he drew upon those experiences to write. To create characters, he used the mannerisms, gestures, speaking styles, and habits he had observed in the customers who came to his uncle's drugstore. The Southern stories were liberally sprinkled with pharmaceutical and medical words, such as *pestle*, *tonic*, and *tinctures*. He wrote his first Southern story in 1896, and by 1910 had published twenty-eight with a Southern setting, excluding Texas and the Southwest.

O. Henry was a well-known writer by the time this photograph was taken in the early 1900s. (Courtesy of the Greensboro Historical Museum.)

During the time O. Henry grew up in North Carolina, the southern states were beginning to leave behind the ways of the Old South that had been shattered by the Civil War. He grew up in the Reconstruction era, when federal law, and sometimes federal troops, concentrated on changing the social structure of the former Confederacy. It was a bitter time for many in the South, particularly those who resisted what they saw as northern efforts to force racial integration.

For the most part, however, O. Henry's stories avoid dealing with these issues. Eight of his tall tales, although set in the South, deal with highly improbable adventures that could have occurred anywhere. Six of them appeared in *The Gentle Grafter*, a collection of fourteen stories told to O. Henry by other inmates while he made his nightly rounds dispensing medicines at the Ohio Penitentiary. These stories generally developed the theme that there was not much difference between the crooks serving time for theft and well respected financiers who cheated people out of their money. It was the only volume of his stories written as a collection. His other volumes were collected reprints of stories previously published in newspapers or magazines.

It was also the only collection that had a central character, Jeff Peters, featured in all but three of the stories. Jeff Peters, the eponymous "Gentle Grafter," thus became O. Henry's most fully developed character. His dialogue carries the stories forward, and much of the humor comes from his frequent malapropisms, or unintentional misuse or distortion of words:

> "There's something we overlooked. The boys ought
> to have dromedaries."
> "What's that?" Andy asks.
> "Why, something to sleep in, of course," says I. "All
> colleges have 'em."

In this case, the speaker means to say dormitories but says dromedaries, or camels, instead.

The humor flows from ridiculous predicaments, or from the actions of con men and swindlers. Almost all of the stories, including one of O. Henry's all-time reader favorites, "The Ransom of Red Chief," conclude with O. Henry's

trademark surprise ending. Two men kidnap a rich man's
son, hoping the father will pay a large ransom for his return.
But the boy soon makes the men regret taking him. In the
end they are willing not only to forgo the ransom, but even
to pay the father to take the boy back:

> Gentlemen: I received your letter to-day by post, in
> regard to the ransom you ask for the return of my son.
> I think you are a little high in your demands, and I
> hereby make you a counter-proposition, which I am
> inclined to believe you will accept. You bring Johnny
> home and pay me two hundred and fifty dollars in
> cash, and I agree to take him off your hands. You had
> better come at night, for the neighbors believe he is
> lost, and I couldn't be responsible for what they
> would do to anybody they saw bringing him back.
> Very respectfully,
> E_____ D_____.

A *New York Times* reviewer called the entire book "something vital, warm and human that commands your liking."

The second category of O. Henry's Southern stories, the
local color romance, uses a close relationship between
setting and character motivation to drive the plot. To avoid
an overdose of sentimentality, O. Henry uses a light irony
that reveals both an admiration for, as well as a critical
appraisal of, a bygone era. However, he avoids a deep
analysis of the characters. It is his sharp description and
skillful dialogue that bring realism to the local color stories.
These tales illustrate his ability to recreate, through dialogue and narrative, what he remembered about his North

The Saturday Evening Post magazine from July 6, 1907, advertises the publication of "The Ransom of Red Chief." This O. Henry short story was later adapted as a movie. (Courtesy of the Austin Public Library.)

Carolina experiences. The local color stories were among his earliest and were mostly written while he was in prison and published soon after his release.

Several of the stories, romantic adventures, display O. Henry's inventiveness at plot development as he skillfully manipulates details to spark the reader's curiosity. "A Retrieved Reformation" was one such story and later became a huge financial success when turned into a play.

Six of his stories blend local color and tall tales and are sometimes farcical or satirical. Many of these stories came later in O. Henry's career, after he had learned how to blend the two types of writing, usually by the use of dialogue and dialect. However, three of the tales were among his earliest stories, probably written in prison or in Pittsburgh.

The "Southern stories" present a combination of the qualities that made O. Henry a popular writer of short fiction: his love of the exotic, the exaggerated, and the picturesque; his awareness of the distinctive differences between the aims of Northerners and Southerners; and his sympathy for changing Southern attitudes and lifestyles.

O. Henry's first big break came in the fall of 1903 when Joseph Pulitzer's *New York World* offered him a contract to produce one story a week at a hundred dollars per story. Half a million people read the *World*, a huge audience. However, O. Henry was still careful to keep his identity unknown. As one friend commented, his secret "became a prison quite as limiting as the walls of the penitentiary." Another friend said, "He shrank from the extended hand of stranger; blushed at spoken approval and avoided conversations about himself." In fact, he stayed so much to himself that few people actually knew where he lived.

This turn of the century New York cityscape shows "Newspaper Row," where many of the country's national newspapers and magazines were published. The New York World *building is on the left with the gold dome.* (Library of Congress)

A college student once tried to capitalize on the O. Henry mystery. The young man's uncle, who was supporting the student, chastised him for falling behind in his studies. The student claimed the reason he had not kept up his grades was because he was the author of the O. Henry stories. When the young man "revealed" himself, one of the leading New York magazines requested a story from him. Of course, he was unable to produce the yarn and had to admit his deception. When someone at *Ainslee's* later told O. Henry about the college student, he simply commented: "Just make sure you send all O. Henry checks to me."

O. Henry was not above a little harmless deceit himself. Mabel Wagnalls, daughter of one of the partners in the publishing firm of Funk & Wagnalls, wrote O. Henry a letter praising the story "Roads of Destiny" and asked for details of his previous career. He responded: "Since you have been so good as to speak nicely of my poor wares I will set down my autobiography. Here goes! Texas cowboy. Lazy. Thought writing stories might be easier than 'busting' broncos. Came to New York one year ago to earn bread, butter, jam, and possibly asparagus that way."

They continued their correspondence while Mabel visited her grandmother in Lithopolis, Ohio. O. Henry met the young lady several times, but they both found more pleasure in their correspondence, seven letters of which she published after his death as *Letters to Lithopolis*.

O. Henry once told his publisher Gilman Hall: "I would like to live a lifetime on each street in New York. Every house has a drama in it." He developed a fascination with the New York working girl, a type that to him represented the modern woman of the new twentieth century. While trying to gather more information about shop girls, he became friends with Anne Partlan, an attractive, thirty-year-old woman who worked for an advertising agency and wrote short stories about the working class as a hobby.

When the two shared their experiences in New York, O. Henry told Anne about his poverty when he first came to the big city. He repeated what he had told Mabel Wagnalls in one of his letters to her: "No one who has not known it can imagine the misery of poverty. Poverty is so terrible and so common, we should all do more than we do— much more—to relieve it."

He told her of a time soon after coming to the city when he could not continue writing because of the delicious cooking aroma coming from a nearby apartment. He was so hungry he started pacing up and down the hallway in front of the apartment door until a girl came out and asked if he had eaten supper already. She said she had more stew than she could eat and that it would not keep. She invited him to share her meal of hazlett stew, made from a calf's liver, kidneys, and heart. Over the meal, she told him about her job curling feathers for wealthy women's hats. Sometime later, after he received payment for a short story, O. Henry knocked on the girl's door to invite her to dinner, but she had moved out. The incident later became the basis for one of his best-known stories, "The Furnished Room," in which he uses "odor" as a crucial element in the story:

> Then suddenly, as he rested there, the room was filled with the strong, sweet odor of mignonette. It came as upon a single buffet of wind with such sureness and fragrance and emphasis that it almost seemed a living visitant. And the man cried aloud: "What, dear?" as if he had been called, and sprang up and faced about. The rich odor clung to him and wrapped him around. He reached out his arms for it, all his senses for the time confused and commingled. How could one be peremptorily called by an odor?

O. Henry asked Anne to let him meet some of her friends without identifying him as the popular author. He listened to their problems with sympathy and understanding. In the summer of 1904 he began a series of "shop girl" stories that became so popular that a critic wrote: "Across the counter of every New York department store is the shadow of O. Henry." Many years later, President Theodore Roosevelt said, "All the reforms that I attempted on behalf of the working girls of New York were suggested by the writings of O. Henry." One of the tales was "An Unfinished Story," with its poignant portrayal of the impoverished shop girl Dulcie:

> Dulcie worked in a department store. She sold Hamburg edging, or stuffed peppers, or automobiles, or other little trinkets such as they keep in department stores. Of what she earned, Dulcie received six dollars per week. . . . I will tell you how she lived on six dollars per week. . . .

> Dulcie hurried homeward. . . . It was Friday; and she had fifty cents left of her week's wages. . . . Dulcie stopped in a store where goods were cheap and bought an imitation lace collar with her fifty cents. That money was to have been spent otherwise— fifteen cents for supper, ten cents for breakfast, ten cents for lunch. Another dime was to be added to her small store of savings; and five cents was to be squandered for licorice drops. . . . The licorice was an extravagance . . . but what is life without pleasures?

An early nineteenth century photograph of New York's Gramercy Park, with Irving Place in the foreground. O. Henry lived here from 1903 to 1907. (Library of Congress)

. . . For the room, Dulcie paid two dollars per week. On week-days her breakfast cost ten cents; she made coffee and cooked an egg over the gaslight while she was dressing. On Sunday mornings she feasted royally on veal chops and pineapple fritters at "Billy's" restaurant, at a cost of twenty-five cents—and tipped the waitress ten cents. New York presents so many temptations for one to run into extravagance.

As O. Henry's own income rose, he began to live in the style he had always wanted. He moved to 55 Irving Place in Gramercy Park, an area of fine restaurants and fancy hotels, as well as saloons, dives, dance halls, and vaudeville theaters. He had enough money to make him welcome among upper society, but he socialized with a small group of acquaintances from the magazine world. He remained reserved, cautious, and furtive, while sitting for hours in the cafes and bars, absorbing the atmosphere and observing the people who would become characters in his stories. He spent a great deal of money on liquor for himself and others.

O. Henry missed his daughter Margaret but felt she was better off living with her grandparents in Pittsburgh than with him in New York. He also worried that if he brought Margaret to New York, someone he had known in prison might recognize him and she would learn his secret. He went to visit his daughter during the summers and wrote her weekly. He wanted Margaret to have a good education and worked to provide her every possible educational advantage.

O. Henry continued to roam the streets of the city, gathering ideas for his mostly sentimental stories about the working class. He based his characters on people he had known and observed in Greensboro, Texas, Honduras, prison, Pittsburgh, and New York. Editors competed for his stories. He had to produce constantly to meet the demand. Yellow pads covered the desk where, with a needle-point lead pencil, he produced 120 new stories in 1904-05.

Fear of discovery remained O. Henry's main preoccupation. He worked harder to conceal his former imprisonment than he did to meet his editors' deadlines. Most of his friends knew that his name was William Sydney Porter, but they did not know that he had been in prison. Early in 1904, the *Critic,* a magazine that was not widely read, claimed that it had discovered the true name of O. Henry, which they said was Sydney Porter. The article included a picture of

Porter taken when he lived in Austin. Several months later, O. Henry received a letter from Judge Robert Hill, the Houston *Post's* publisher, who had provided two hundred dollars to help with Porter's trial expenses— money Porter used to travel to Honduras. Hill had recognized O. Henry's picture in the *Critic*.

The contents of the letter are unknown but must have been friendly based upon O. Henry's reply, which described his quiet lifestyle, his desire not to advertise his past, and the forthcoming publication of his first book. He wrote: "My book will bring me in some money, and with the first surplus over my living expenses I intend to settle some old debts. Yours I have not by any means forgotten, and it comes among the first." Apparently, no one in New York made the connection of Sydney Porter to an ex-convict.

As O. Henry sold story after story with a Central American setting to various New York magazines, Witter Bynner, a young editor at *McClure's*, suggested turning the Central American stories into a novel. Novels sold better than short story collections. Bynner proposed making each story a chapter and tying them together with a narrative thread. O. Henry agreed, and the two men began cutting and pasting. Using the short story "Money Maze" as the plot basis, they divided the story into segments that were attached to pieces of other stories. All but two or three of the chapters were carved out of seven previously published stories edited slightly to include chapter headings and to change some character and place names. To fill out the novel, titled *Cabbages and Kings*, O. Henry wrote some additional stories. In the end, the book contained nineteen chapters.

The plot thread concerned the theft of the national treasury of the fictional Republic of Anchuria and revolved around two presidents. One was the absconding Anchurian president Miraflores, and the other was an American embezzler, President Wahrfield of the Republic Insurance Company, who was hiding out in Anchuria. Most of the stories in the collection fell into the category of tall tales in which remembered fact and fanciful invention were closely woven together. Although O. Henry often captured realistic surface details in these stories, they do not represent his experiences in Honduras, but create a fantasy world loosely based on what he saw and heard there.

O. Henry told his readers what to expect when he opened the story "The World and the Door" with these lines: "A favorite dodge to get your story read by the public is to assert that it is true, and then add that Truth is stranger than Fiction." When he gave a double twist to the story's end, his readers could not complain. They had been warned.

Cabbages and Kings introduces almost every characteristic that O. Henry developed in his later stories: a bit of philosophy, illumination of a character with a few well-chosen details, the use of diverting quotations, the pitting of one city against another, calculated exaggeration, and beautiful description. It was the last feature that caught reviewers' eyes. They praised such realistic passages as the description of Coralio, the port capital of the mythical Republic of Anchuria:

The mountains reached up their bulky shoulders to receive the level gallop of Apollo's homing steeds, the day died in the lagoons and in the shadowed banana groves and in the mangrove swamps, where the great blue crabs were beginning to crawl to land for their nightly ramble. And it died, at last, upon the highest peaks. Then the brief twilight, ephemeral as the flight of a moth, came and went; the Southern Cross peeped with its topmost eye above a row of palms, and the fire-flies heralded with their torches the approach of soft-footed night.

McClure, Phillips, & Co. published *Cabbages and Kings* on November 28, 1904, and promoted it with an exaggerated claim about O. Henry's expertise on Central America: "The author, who has lived many years among the people of the South American republics, draws upon his fund of experience in this breezy story which recounts the adventures of an energetic American in the land of popular revolutions." Although the book received some good reviews, it was not the financial success that O. Henry and *McClure's* had hoped it would be. The most favorable review came from Stanhope Searles in the *Bookman*:

With his stories of life in the Central American republics Mr. Henry ... [portrays the characters] with much humour and sympathy and keenness, and behind them you are made to see that wonderful background of white beach and waving palms and sunshine and flowers and fruit and dirt and discomfort. ... *Cabbages and Kings* is a book of very unusual interest and cleverness.

An early 1900s ad promoting O. Henry's work in McClure's. *(UNC Greensboro)*

O. Henry had hit his stride as a writer, but he still had economic problems, many brought about by his generosity to anyone who asked him for money. One time he stood on a New York street corner while he talked to a friend. A beggar approached the two and asked for money. O. Henry slipped a coin into the beggar's hand and said, "Here's a dollar. Don't bother us any more." The beggar walked a few steps away, looked at the coin and then back at his benefactor. He returned and said, "I don't want to take advantage of you. You said this was a dollar. It's a twenty-dollar gold piece." O. Henry told him, "Don't you think I know what a dollar is? I told you not to come back!" He continued his conversation with his friend.

At other times O. Henry would go to a local restaurant where he would exchange a twenty-dollar bill for eighty quarters. Then after dinner he strolled through Madison Park, handing out them out to the homeless people sleeping on the benches, roaming the streets until the quarters were gone. Such generosity, along with his living expenses and his steady drinking, kept him in financial trouble.

In 1905 he signed a contract with *Munsey's Magazine*, giving them the right of first refusal on all his stories. They agreed to pay ten cents a word for all the stories they published. Under this arrangement, some of his stories paid as much as five hundred dollars, but the usual payment was $250 to $350. Keeping up this production schedule began to wear on O. Henry's health, and his pace slowed.

Sometimes under pressure from an editor, O. Henry would give them a title to promote the story and then hurry to write it in the next few hours before press time. He could conceive a story idea in a flash, but putting it down on paper required great effort. He tried to get a story complete in his mind before starting to write. Once he had committed the story to paper, he mailed it immediately to an editor without revision. In an interview with George MacAdam of the *New York Sunday Times*, he said: "You can't write a story that's got any life in it by sitting at a writing table and thinking. You've got to get out into the streets, into the crowds, talk with people, and feel the rush and throb of real life—that's the stimulant for a story writer."

O. Henry kept going by juggling various editors' requests and meeting the demands of the most persistent first. By 1905-06, his salary was six hundred dollars a month, a good income for that time. Yet he was always in debt and constantly asked for advances. Most of his editors complied with his requests. They provided him the same type of support he had received in earlier years from the Halls, the Harrells, the Andersons, the Roaches, and many in the Ohio State Penitentiary.

To cope with his stressful, deadline-oriented life, he began to turn more and more to alcohol. He would sometimes have a drink before breakfast. He moved frequently until finally settling at the Caledonia Hotel, where he virtually barricaded himself in his room. But, despite his attempt to hide, he was about to enter a new phase in his life.

SEVEN

SECOND MARRIAGE

When O. Henry had left Greensboro to go to Texas, he lost touch with his first love, Sara Coleman, the "Sallie" of his youth. Sara had never married and, after not seeing him for many years, she began to hear rumors that "O. Henry" was the Will Porter she had once known. Sara had always wanted to be a writer and decided to contact O. Henry. She sent him a letter in care of *Everybody's Magazine*, in which she had read several of his stories.

O. Henry responded quickly and warmly:

> My dear "Miss Sally":
> Just once, if I may, and then I'll try to think of you as "Sara." I was gladder to get your little note than the biggest editor's check I ever saw. Seems to me . . . I do remember a small, "sassy" girl that used to visit Aunt "Bert." . . . I never expected anything so

nice and jolly as to hear from you. It's like finding
a $5 bill in an old vest pocket. . . . I'd be pleased to
hear from you. . .

Sincerely yours,

W. S. Porter

They corresponded for a year. O. Henry tried to find a
buyer for some of Sara's stories and told her that if she
wanted to become a writer she should move to, or at least

*In this letter to Sara, O. Henry playfully references his childhood memory of
her preference for magnolias.* (Courtesy of the Greensboro Historical Museum.)

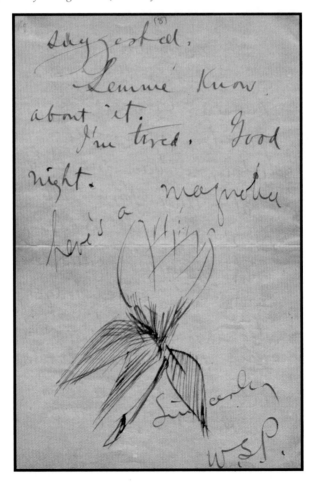

visit, New York. Sara did not immediately respond to the suggestion.

In April 1906, O. Henry's second book was published. *The Four Million* was a collection of twenty-five stories previously printed in the *World*. The title came in response to a list put together some years back naming the cream of New York society. The number four hundred represented the capacity of wealthy socialite Mrs. William B. Astor's ballroom. O. Henry wrote, "Not very long ago some one invented the assertion that there were only 'Four Hundred' people in New York City who were really worth noticing. But a wiser man has arisen—the census taker—and his larger estimate of human interest has been preferred in marking out the field of these little stories of the 'Four Million.' "This egalitarian outlook struck a chord with people everywhere. The book was popular and included some of O. Henry's best known stories, including "The Cop and the Anthem" and "The Gift of the Magi."

The latter story came about in a typically spontaneous manner. The *World* had requested one of his stories for its Christmas issue. It was to be used as the centerpiece of the magazine section and would be illustrated in color. Using color meant that the illustrations must be ready earlier than usual, and the text of the story must be set in type before the rest of the section. A struggle ensued between author and editor. When the deadline passed and there was still no story, the newspaper editors sent the illustrator Dan Smith to see if O. Henry could give him at least an idea to help him get started on the illustrations.

O. Henry hesitated, staring out his window. Finally, he told Smith: "I'll tell you what you do, Colonel. Just draw a picture of a poorly furnished room, the kind you find in a boarding house or rooming house over on the West Side. In the room there is only a chair or two, a chest of drawers, a bed, and a trunk. On the bed, a man and a girl are sitting side by side. They are talking about Christmas. The man has a watch fob in his hand. He is playing with it while he is thinking. The girl's principal feature is the long beautiful hair that is hanging down her back. That's all I can think of now. But the story is coming."

Later that morning, when a friend, Lindsey Denison, stopped by for a visit, O. Henry said to him, "Lie down there on the sofa. Have to have a story done this afternoon. I've thought of an idea but I need a living model. I am going to write about you and your wife. I've never met her, but I think that you two are the kind that would make sacrifices for each other. Now stay on the sofa and don't interrupt." Within three hours, he had written "The Gift of the Magi," the story of Della and James, a poverty-stricken couple living in a one-room apartment in New York at Christmas time. To buy a chain for her husband's pocket watch, Della cuts and sells her beautiful long hair. James, ironically, sells his watch to buy a set of combs for his wife's hair. The story ends with the recognition that the couple's physical possessions pale in comparison to the unselfish love they share.

Shortly after the publication of *The Four Million*, seventeen-year-old Margaret finally went to New York to see her father. The two had a wonderful visit. O. Henry

O. Henry's story, "Gift of the Magi," appeared in the December 10, 1905, issue of the New York World. (Courtesy of Rare Book, Manuscript, and Special Collections Library, Duke University.)

playfully called Margaret "Bill" or sometimes "Jim" or "Pete." She called him "Colonel." As they strolled about Long Island,

Margaret confided that she did not want to go to college. This deeply disappointed O. Henry, who had long dreamed of his daughter getting a top-notch education.

After Margaret's visit, O. Henry continued to gather the stories that would eventually appear in *The Trimmed Lamp*, his second collection of New York stories. When the volume appeared in 1907, it drew hearty endorsements from the critics. An *Atlantic Monthly* reviewer wrote that "The reader who skips a single story in the collection runs the risk of losing something that he would have liked quite as well as those he read if not rather better."

In the late summer of that year, with $150 earned from her own writing, Sara Coleman decided to visit some friends in Boston. She wrote to O. Henry that she would stop over in New York for a few days on her way back, and he made arrangements for her to stay with the Gilman Halls. Sara and O. Henry saw each other for the first time since childhood on September 11, his forty-fifth birthday.

O. Henry barely recognized Sara, now a handsome woman with dark, strong features. During her visit, he treated her like a queen. Although he did not have Judge Tourgée's magnolias for her in New York, he did send her a steady flow of American beauty roses during her stay. A cab waited for her whenever she wanted to go out, and she received excellent service at all of the restaurants because O. Henry had tipped the waiters in advance. O. Henry felt young again and bragged to Sara that he had only begun the great things he would do in writing.

At first he did not realize that if Sara had heard rumors

connecting him to O. Henry, she might have also heard he was an ex-convict. He knew Sara came from a strict Presbyterian family, and he feared what she might do if she learned he had a prison record. He decided to tell her only if their relationship reached a point where he felt Sara would accept his marriage proposal. When the time finally came, he was so shaken with embarrassment that all he could tell her was that he had concealed something about himself that could prevent her from wanting to marry him. He promised to write to her when she returned to North Carolina and tell her the full story.

Expecting never to see or hear from Sara again, O. Henry kept his promise and wrote her a letter containing all of the details of his Texas trial and his subsequent imprisonment. Her response to his confession has never been found. However, they continued to exchange letters, in which he told her that he needed her and that together they could build a home. But the proud O. Henry also said he did not want Sara to accept him as damaged goods or marked-down merchandise. He wanted her to see him as either a good person or a bad person, nothing in between. After a while, he visited Sara and her family in Asheville, North Carolina, and the two set a wedding date for November 27, 1907.

Porter invited Gilman Hall to serve as his best man at the wedding and asked him to help with some of the arrangements. He wanted Hall to buy a narrow wedding band, size 5 1/8, from Tiffany's and to order two special bouquets from a New York florist—lilies of the valley and pale pink roses. The Reverend R. F. Campbell performed the ceremony in

O. Henry and Sara on their honeymoon in western North Carolina. (Courtesy of the Greensboro Historical Museum.)

Asheville and the couple honeymooned in nearby Hot Springs.

However, the marriage had little chance of success. She had never married and he had been alone for so long that they could not adjust to each other's fixed habits. Sara disliked the strain of living in hotels and apartments and having their income shift from wealth one day to poverty the next. Supporting a wife increased the financial pressure, and O. Henry pushed himself even harder. But even the $14,000 he made in 1908 could not support their grand lifestyle.

O. Henry's latest collection, *The Heart of the West,* was published the month before his wedding. The book contained stories based mainly on O. Henry's experiences in Texas, including "An Afternoon Miracle," the revised title for his first big sale, "The Miracle of Lava Canyon." From his Texas experiences, which included his time at the sheep ranch, the land office, the bank in Austin, and the Houston *Post*, O. Henry gathered enough raw material for about eighty stories, not including those published in *The Rolling Stone* or the Houston *Post*.

One of the most distinguishing characteristics of his Texas stories is setting. A passage from "Hygeia at the Solito" illustrates his ability to describe vividly both the physical appearance of something, and the atmosphere, using a minimum of well-selected sensory details.

> They sped upon velvety wheels across an exhilarant savanna. The pair of Spanish ponies struck a nimble, tireless trot, which gait they occasionally relieved by a wild, untrammelled gallop. The air was wine and seltzer, perfumed, as they absorbed it, with the delicate redolence of prairie flowers. The road perished, and the buckboard swam the uncharted billows of the grass itself.

The freedom of movement in this land of wide-open spaces also provided hiding places for bands of outlaws that brought fear and destruction in their wake. O. Henry created more than 250 characters for his Texas stories, but the characters were not as well developed as the settings. Most of the characters are men and are one-dimensionally either good or bad. Yet these archetypes assume a multitude of vocations, such as bankers, burglars, cattle kings, clerks, cooks, cowboys, doctors, farmers, hoboes, outlaws, rangers, sheep men, and station agents.

O. Henry also repeats the same motifs in a variety of situations. For example, the boy-meets-girl situation might result from rivalry, pride, misunderstanding, mistaken identity, or some combination thereof. Another popular motif is the reformation or rehabilitation of a character. Occasionally, O. Henry brings into conflict the forces of crime and the law. His favorite character model for authority was Lee Hall, the former Texas Ranger on the Dull Ranch, where he had lived for several years. Other common motifs include vindication and self-sacrifice.

Eastern reviewers did not like these Texas tall tales as much as they did the New York stories. Many of them had never been west of the Hudson River and could not distinguish between truth and fiction because O. Henry was so adept at mixing real adventures with make-believe. They considered the Texas stories cheaply clever and grossly exaggerated. A reviewer for the *Nation* wrote: "Mr. Porter's new volume of short stories is a distinct disappointment. . . . His Texan cow punchers talk like intoxicated dictionaries. . . . At a time when such quality as he has shown is rare, Mr. Porter must take that talent a trifle more seriously."

As he received the reviews of his latest book, O. Henry tried to hold together some semblance of family life. Having completed finishing school, eighteen-year-old Margaret joined her father and Sara, but her presence caused more strain on the new marriage. Because of the tense atmosphere, O. Henry kept a small apartment where he could write undisturbed while the family spent the summer in a cottage at Good Ground, Long Island.

The money problems continued. O. Henry invited a new magazine editor to spend the weekend with them on Long Island, but he did not have enough money to buy groceries. He woke up early before the visitor arrived, sat at his desk, and wrote for three hours. By noon he had sold the story by telephone and rushed it over to *Munsey's Magazine*, where he received three hundred dollars.

In May 1908 Porter's third collection of New York stories, *The Voice of the City*, was published. Critics received this book more favorably than they had *The Heart of the West*. The book showed the author's knowledge of the city and his love of its people. A review in *Outlook* stated: "A new book of stories about New York by O. Henry is sure of a welcome."

By the end of the summer, the Porters essentially gave up on the marriage. Sara returned to Asheville for an indefinite visit, and Margaret enrolled for the winter term at a private school in Edgewood, New Jersey. O. Henry returned to his bachelor ways at the Hotel Caledonia. In November, *The Gentle Grafter*, O. Henry's book of stories about society's misfits, received favorable reviews. *The New York Times Book Review* said that "His creations are so true to human nature that no matter how strange their dialect or unfamiliar their appearance, neither this unfamiliarity nor this strangeness strikes you as you read—it is the humanity which we all share that comes home."

Ironically, the more praise he received, the more O. Henry criticized himself. He expressed his lack of satisfaction to a friend: "I'm a failure. I always have the feeling that I want to get back somewhere, but I don't know just where it is. My stories? No, they don't satisfy me. . . . It depresses me to have people point me out or introduce me as 'a celebrated author.' It seems such a big label for such picayune goods." He wanted to write more serious stories and planned a whole series contrasting the Old South and the New South. "I want to show the public that I can write something new—new for me, I mean—a story without slang, a straightforward dramatic plot treated in a way that will come nearer my ideal of real story-writing." He outlined the series and sold the idea to *Collier's*, but never wrote the stories.

O. Henry also planned a serious novel and convinced his publishers, Doubleday, Page & Company, to give him several generous cash advances on the book. However, while supposedly working on it, he was collaborating with Franklin R. Adams to compose a musical comedy called *Lo!* based on one of his 1908 stories, "To Him Who Waits." The play opened in Aurora, Illinois, in August but never made it to the New York stage, folding during the road tryouts after fourteen performances, none of which O. Henry saw.

The comedy did catch the attention of another theatrical producer, George Tyler, who approached O. Henry about converting his short story "A Retrieved Reformation" into a play. Although he needed the money, O. Henry declined but agreed to sell the rights for five hundred dollars. When asked to define a play, O. Henry replied that "A play is something that I can't write." Another writer, Paul Armstrong, later turned the story into a play called *Alias Jimmy Valentine* that was an immediate hit and brought in $100,000 in royalties in its first year. When later asked about whether or not he regretted selling the rights to his story, O. Henry replied: "Not at all. When a dramatist puts a kick into one of my stories and gets his money back I am tickled along my entire vertebrae."

During the time that O. Henry worked on the play and talked about a serious novel, Doubleday, Page & Company, his new publishers, brought out his next collection, *Roads of Destiny*, a combination of Texas, New Orleans, and Central American stories. The volume had been assembled somewhat haphazardly and lacked a unifying theme. Reviews were mixed, and it brought in relatively modest revenue.

In the fall of 1909, O. Henry visited Sara in Asheville, hoping that the fresh mountain air and climbing the

O. Henry on vacation in the North Carolina mountains in 1909. (Courtesy of the Greensboro Historical Museum.)

North Carolina hills would cure a nagging cough. He also suffered from diabetes, and his work was frustrating him. He wanted to write something longer than a short story, but, although he had ideas for a novel and a play, he could not get the words to paper. "I want to get at something bigger," he said. "What I have done is child's play to what I can do, to what I know it is in me to do." But he could not get started. He told Sara: "I could look at these mountains a hundred years and never get an idea, but just one block downtown and I catch a sentence, see something in a face—and I've got my story."

O. Henry had employed his friend Seth Moyle, a New York agent, to handle some of his literary affairs. Moyle presented the next proposed collection to publishers on a best-offer basis. In October a new publisher, Harper Brothers, published *Options*, a book of sixteen stories O. Henry had written in the past two years. Again reviews were mixed. *Nation* called O. Henry's structural cleverness his "darker angel" and found nothing new to praise about the collection. Although a *New York Times* reviewer somewhat agreed, he also wrote that the book was "full of good stories—wonderfully good stories of men and women—most of them still rather young—stories that flash upon you things which your stupidity and inattention has missed when you have looked with your own uncoached eyes upon the identical common life they are concerned to picture."

The creative muse deserted O. Henry in North Carolina. After six restless months, he returned to New York. He wrote his former Texas business partner, "I'm back in New York after a six months' stay in the mountains near Asheville, North Carolina. I was all played out—nerves, etc. I thought I was much better and came back to New York about a month ago and have been in bed most of the time— didn't pick up down there as well as I should have done. There was too much scenery and fresh air. What I need is a steam-heated flat and no ventilation or exercise."

In March 1910 a new collection, *Strictly Business*, was published. Most of the stories had been previously printed in the Sunday *World*. While still in North Carolina, O. Henry had planned this collection with Harry Payton Steger, editor at Doubleday. Though it contained what many consider his finest story, "A Municipal Report," and some of his other best-known stories, the reviews were lukewarm. Critics again described the book, like several previous collections, as uneven and hastily put together. *Nation's* reviewer wrote that the book had added twenty-three chapters to O. Henry's "encyclopaedic account of the impudence, the energy, the recklessness, the vulgar loves, the fat and cynical materialism of proletarian America." This was the last book published during O. Henry's lifetime.

O. Henry's health continued to decline. Anne Partlan visited him at the Caledonia. He refused to leave his room. Agonizing pains gripped his body on the evening of June 3, 1910. He started to call his friend Gilman Hall but remembered that Mrs. Hall was expecting to deliver a baby at any time. He called Anne instead. When she answered the phone, she heard him say, "I'm sick, Anne. I need help."

The last known picture taken of O. Henry before his death. He had gained more than fifty pounds since his release from prison. (Doubleday & Co.)

Anne told him to call his doctor and started for his hotel. O. Henry managed to reach his physician, an osteopath, but Anne arrived before the doctor and found O. Henry semiconscious on the floor, the telephone dangling from the receiver as if he had collapsed right after calling her for help. When the doctor arrived, he took one look at O. Henry and said he could not handle that kind of case.

Frantic, Anne called Charles Russell Hancock, a friend as well as a surgeon, who came immediately. He wanted to call an ambulance to take O. Henry to the Polyclinic Hospital on East Thirty-fourth Street, but O. Henry refused because he did not have enough money. It would take thirty dollars to get him admitted, and O. Henry had only twenty-three cents in his pocket. Dr. Hancock left to try to make arrangements to have him admitted into the hospital.

Anne had left home so quickly that she had not brought her purse. She dashed out to ask some friends who lived nearby to lend her the money. As she ran out of the hotel, she saw Mr. Miller, manager of the Caledonia. Anne explained the situation, and Mr. Miller gave her the thirty dollars. O. Henry and Anne then took a cab to the hospital.

At the hospital, O. Henry was determined that no one would know his real name. He told Anne to use "Dennis," an old Texas name meaning "disastrous things to come," as his first name when she registered him. When she refused to use such a discouraging name, he asked her to give "Parker" as his last name. Anne agreed and told the hospital officials that the patient was Will S. Parker.

The doctors at the hospital found multiple medical problems—cirrhosis of the liver, diabetes, and an enlarged heart. O. Henry had been in the hospital a couple of days when a nurse came into his room to care for him at about midnight. As she left the room, she started to turn off the lights. With a smile, O. Henry uttered words from a popular song of the day, "Turn up the lights; I don't want to go home in the dark." The next morning at 7:06 on June 5, 1910, William Sydney Porter, alias O. Henry, died, three months shy of his forty-eighth birthday.

Gilman Hall and two other editors made arrangements for a brief funeral service at the Little Church Around the Corner on West Twenty-Ninth Street. Twelve hours after her husband's death, Sara arrived in New York. Porter had made no attempt to notify her of the seriousness of his condition; she was expecting him to come to Asheville for a visit later that month. Only a handful of relatives and people from the literary world attended the services. Among them were Mabel Wagnalls, his correspondent in *Letters to Lithopolis*, and her mother. Most of the reading public made no connection between William Sydney Porter and the writer O. Henry.

An O. Henry-esque surprise ending occurred even at his funeral. The church had made an error and scheduled a wedding at the same time as the funeral. The groom's brother arrived early for the wedding only to find funeral preparations underway. As the best man, he did not want the bride-to-be to hear about the mix-up. He met the bridal party at the curb when they arrived at the church and explained that the church had slipped another wedding in ahead of theirs. He said that he had rescheduled their wedding for noon and suggested the entire party go to a nearby hotel to wait.

When the wedding party left, O. Henry's funeral began. Because the funeral started late, the bridal party arrived back at the church before the end of the service. Those inside the church could hear the happy chatter of the bridal party out in the garden at the same time they listened to the solemn funeral.

O. Henry's body was taken to Pennsylvania Station and sent to Asheville, where the same minister who had married him and Sara in 1907 conducted the graveside services. He was buried in the Riverside Cemetery overlooking the French Broad River. His granite tombstone simply read "William Sydney Porter 1862-1910." There was no mention of O. Henry, who died owing thousands of dollars advanced to him by publishers and friends.

EIGHT

AN ENIGMA

O. Henry's popularity as a writer continued to grow even after his death. He was compared to American writers Edgar Allan Poe and Mark Twain and to British author Rudyard Kipling. In 1908 a *North American Review* essay compared him favorably to the famous French short-story writer Guy de Maupassant. O. Henry became the "Yankee Maupassant," a nickname that his publishers used liberally in their advertising. Between 1910 and 1915, numerous essays about O. Henry and his work appeared in such magazines as *Bookman*, *Cosmopolitan*, and *Current Opinion*. Hildegarde Hawthorne, writing for the *New York Times* on June 18, 1910, said that "His [O. Henry's] style was perfect; it was the man himself; nervous, picturesque, quick, supple, with easy, inevitable metaphors."

To increase sales and recover some advance money,

Guy de Maupassant

Guy de Maupassant, the French short story writer, was born on August 5, 1850, probably at the Chateau de Miromesniel near the French seacoast town of Dieppe. He received his early education from his mother. Growing up in Normandy, Maupassant enjoyed outdoor sports and fishing. His parents separated when he was eleven years old, and he and his younger brother Hervé lived with their mother, whom Maupassant adored. At the age of thirteen, he enrolled in a seminary but managed to get himself expelled for his disobedience. From there he was sent to a school in Paris to prepare to study law. His gift of a photographic memory allowed him to store large amounts of detailed information that later found its way into his stories of the Normandy people.

Guy de Maupassant.

However, at the age of twenty, Maupassant left school and enlisted in the French army to serve in the Franco-Prussian War from 1870-1871. After the war, Maupassant worked as a civil servant from 1872-1880, first in the naval department and later in the ministry of education, where he became a contributing editor to several newspapers. In 1880 he published his first masterpiece, a short story titled "Boule de Suif," or "Tallow Ball." The story brought him almost instant recognition.

At first glance, Maupassant's stories appear to be brief anecdotes about simple episodes from everyday life. On closer inspection, however, it can be seen that they are actually deep insights into human character. In 1881, Maupassant published his first volume of short stories, which was reprinted twelve times in the next two years. His stories' clever plots, taken from the Normandy peasant life, the Franco-Prussian War, lives of the middle class, and the fashionable life in Paris, are marked by objectivity, a highly controlled style, and some humor.

During the 1880s Maupassant wrote three hundred short stories, six novels, three travel books, and a book of poetry. His work brought him fame and wealth, but he preferred solitude over society, although he traveled extensively.

Unfortunately, Maupassant had contracted syphilis in his twenties, and the disease eventually affected his mental stability. On January 2, 1892, he attempted suicide by cutting his throat and was committed to a private asylum in Paris, where he died on July 6, 1893, a month short of his forty-third birthday.

Harry Payton Steger publicized the author widely. Steger, literary advisor to Doubleday, had helped put together O. Henry's last book. He had also been named O. Henry's biographer and Margaret's guardian. Steger tried to create an anthology of the popular writer's career, still largely unknown to the reading public at the time of his death. Steger began with fictional anecdotes and sketches published in *The Rolling Stone* in 1894 and with unpublished letters O. Henry wrote from Texas and from prison. Steger then set the letters and sketches against stories written at the peak of O. Henry's career. Interspersed among the writings were pictures of O. Henry at various times and reproductions of his drawings from *The Rolling Stone*.

The first item in *Rolling Stones*, the name Steger gave to the anthology he edited, was a four-page fragment of an unfinished manuscript O. Henry was supposedly working on when he died. This story, titled "Dream," would, according to Steger, have begun a series in a completely new style for O. Henry. Even so, the fragment indicates the story probably would still have ended with O. Henry's trademark surprise ending.

Steger next tried to sell a limited first edition of O. Henry's complete works, 250 printings of twelve volumes at $125 per set. Each volume contained a sheet of yellow paper like the ones used by O. Henry to write his stories. The volumes quickly sold out.

After that, Steger began working on O. Henry's biography, but he died unexpectedly at the age of thirty. The biography was finished by C. Alphonso Smith and published in 1916.

The book was ultimately well received, but Smith's uncritical look at O. Henry drew some negative criticism. However, motion pictures of more than a dozen of his stories, mostly his Texas tales, enchanted huge audiences. Posthumous publication of collections of O. Henry's stories also continued to keep his reputation alive. These included *Sixes and Sevens* (1911), *Rolling Stones* (1912), and *Waifs and Strays* (1917). More than half of *Waifs and Strays* featured critical articles written about O. Henry. These responses from the critics further stimulated public interest.

While his publishers tried to keep O. Henry's reputation afloat, his daughter Margaret wanted to follow in her father's footsteps. She took a writing course at Columbia University and read and reread O. Henry's stories to study his style. O. Henry's editors tried to present her as "Miss O. Henry." However, they soon discovered that she did not possess her father's talent.

In 1916 Margaret married Oscar Cesare, a well-known cartoonist and illustrator, but less than a year later she headed for Reno to get a divorce. In the post World War I era, she found herself in financial straits. She sold all of her jewelry to get enough money to go to Hollywood, where she planned to negotiate with a film studio for rights to her father's stories, but she became seriously ill in the middle of the negotiations.

When doctors told her she had tuberculosis, she collapsed in a heap, shaking and sobbing. She had just started to make progress on her writing, and a publisher had recently accepted some of it. Her doctor insisted that Margaret move to the desert, where she could benefit from the dry winds, the sunshine, and the quiet.

Margaret Porter shortly before her death in 1927. (Courtesy of the Greensboro Historical Museum.)

In a memorial written in 1923 called "My O. Henry," Margaret wrote of her relationship with her father. From childhood until their last meeting in Asheville just before her father's death, Margaret wrote that the relationship "was never that of father and daughter; rather that of two good friends, for never did he give a command, and never did I fail to follow his advice or to try to fulfill his expressed wish."

In order to comply with the doctor's directions, Guy Sartin, a young English writer and a friend, had checked out possible sites in California for Margaret. At his suggestion, she bought a few acres in the California desert near Banning and built a bungalow.

Sartin visited her every day during her two-year illness. Sartin reminded Margaret of her father. She wrote a friend, "God sent him to me. He is more like my father than any other man I've ever known." Sartin also helped her to start writing the "true" biography of her father. She had completed only about half of it when she had a severe coughing attack. Her temperature rose to 101 degrees.

Margaret knew she did not have long to live, so she contacted an attorney to make a will. She asked for a new bed jacket to use as a wedding gown and called a jeweler to bring out a tray of wedding rings. Then she told Sartin, "And now we will be married." A seamstress had sewn a new bed jacket of black lace over pink chiffon. On the day of her wedding, Margaret styled her auburn hair, put on a little makeup, and donned the bed jacket. Sartin gathered roses from Margaret's garden to decorate the bungalow. They invited two or three neighbors to the brief ceremony.

Sartin placed the simple gold wedding ring on Margaret's thumb as she requested. She had told the jeweler to design the ring to fit her husband's finger instead of her own because she knew that she would not live much longer. Three days later, at age thirty-eight, Margaret died.

A local minister conducted her funeral at the Little Church of Flowers in Glendale, California. Her remains were cremated at the Forest Lawn Cemetery in Banning, California, and her ashes were sent to Riverside Cemetery in Asheville, where they were buried at the feet of her beloved father. Margaret's will left all proceeds from her father's literary works to her widower, Guy Sartin, her husband of less than a week.

How much those proceeds would be was an open question. O. Henry's reputation continued to fluctuate. The first annual volume of *O. Henry Memorial Award Prize Stories* appeared in 1919. He had gained an enthusiastic following in England, Russia, France, and other European countries, despite the difficulties of translating his American colloquialisms. By 1920, nearly five million copies of his books had been sold in the United States and a similar number in several other English-speaking countries.

However, in that same decade, other writers, such as Sherwood Anderson and Ernest Hemingway, began to woo critics with a new style of realism. O. Henry's works were attacked as contrived, superficial, and overly sentimental. The new generation of critics went so far as to picture him as someone who had cheapened the short story form. Leading the criticism was Katherine Fullerton Gerould, an

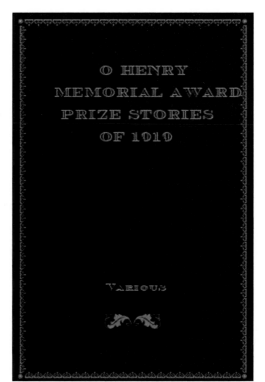

The first edition of the O. Henry prize stories, published in 1919.

admired short story writer, who wrote: "O. Henry did not write the short story. O. Henry wrote the expanded anecdote. In a short story there are situation, suspense, and climax. O. Henry gave the reader climax—nothing else."

The negative reviews brought about counterattacks, such as the one by Stephen Leacock, Canadian humorist and essayist, who said that if O. Henry's stories were only anecdotes, "Let's have another barrelful." He predicted that soon "the whole English-speaking world will recognize in O. Henry one of the great masters of modern literature."

Yet, by the time Margaret died, O. Henry's reputation had declined as quickly as it had risen in previous decades.

Noted newspaperman, book reviewer, and political analyst H. L. Mencken, in his *Prejudices: Second Series*, charged: "In the whole canon of O. Henry's work you will not find a single recognizable character; his people are unanimously marionettes; he makes Mexican brigands, Texas cowmen and New York cracksmen talk the same highly ornate Broadwayese."

By the end of the 1920s few critics or other writers even mentioned O. Henry. They preferred the new fiction that relied more on experimentation with understatement and symbolism than with plot construction. His stories were considered to be outdated. O. Henry seemed doomed to literary oblivion.

These attitudes continued throughout the forties and well into the fifties. The pendulum began gradually to swing back in his favor, however, with the advent of motion picture, stage, and television adaptations. In the mid-1950s the O. Henry Television Playhouse presented more than forty dramatizations, and in the next decade there were 130 motion pictures based on O. Henry stories. In 1958, the Texas Heritage Foundation and the Greensboro Writers Club jointly appealed to President Eisenhower to grant O. Henry a posthumous pardon for his embezzlement conviction, but Eisenhower refused because the president of the United States could not pardon a dead man.

A year later, O. Henry's widow, Sara, died at the age of ninety-one in Asheville. Her burial took place in the Riverside Cemetery, where O. Henry was buried.

In 1962 the Soviet Union, where O. Henry's vigorous,

fresh language and working-class characters were widely appreciated, issued a memorial stamp in his honor. In a new biography in 1965, Eugene Current-Garcia wrote: "To condemn O. Henry's stories *in toto* for not being realistic and serious, for depending too heavily on coincidence, and for playing to the gallery is an evasion of the critic's responsibility—unless it can be shown that these characteristics invariably result in badly written stories. This, O. Henry's severest critics have seldom been willing to do. His intention rather than his achievement has been the object of their censure."

By the 1970s a resurgence of critical studies showed a renewed interest in the short-story writer. In 1985 the citizens of North Carolina erected a life-size bronze statue on the occasion of the seventy-fifth anniversary of O. Henry's death. The Greensboro Public Library retains his family's Bible and his cradle. In Raleigh, the Supreme Court Building bears a plaque commemorating the famous author.

The Victorian-style house in Austin, Texas, where Porter and Athol lived as a young married couple was turned into a museum. In 1999 it received recognition as a national Literary Landmark. The home has not changed much from the years when the Porters lived in it. Visitors can see actual pieces of furniture the Porters used, as well as period pieces typical of that era. O. Henry's writing desk, which originally belonged to Adolphus Stern, personal secretary to Sam Houston when Houston served as president of the Republic of Texas, is in the front room. In San Antonio, the house

he rented when he came to the city to gather news for *The Rolling Stone* has also become a museum.

Now that all of O. Henry's work is in the public domain, it is impossible to gauge his popularity based on the sales of his stories. Although his work has appealed to the mass market for more than a century now, most critics do not place him among the world's great short-story writers. O. Henry admitted that he never revised or rewrote, and often used tricks to make his stories entertaining to as large an audience as possible.

There are literary qualities to O. Henry's stories that have helped to keep them alive long after the world he described, which was so recognizable to many of his readers, particularly in New York, has vanished. He knew what life in America was like for the average person and reproduced it in both a realistic and symbolic manner. His language, attitude, and the prevailing spirit in his stories is quintessentially American, as is his basic human sympathy and pleasure in the common joys and sorrows of life.

Although O. Henry made no conscious effort to effect social change, his stories reflected a new spirit of social consciousness and opened the door to new topics for the short story genre. His use of humor, slang, and the inevitable surprise ending are all trademarks that later writers emulated.

O. Henry remains an enigma, both as a man and as a writer. Many of the highs and lows of this fiercely private

Opposite: *A crowd gathers for the dedication of a plaque honoring O. Henry in front of a house he once occupied in Texas.* (Courtesy of the Greensboro Historical Museum.)

man's life are not reflected in his work. Although O. Henry may not be remembered as a great artist, he never purported to be one. He was, above all else, an entertainer. His work, like his life, is brimming with lively and fanciful tales that continue to appeal to this day.

Timeline

Born on September 11 in Greensboro, North Carolina, the second of three sons.
Mother dies from tuberculosis on September 26.
Starts working in uncle's drugstore at age fifteen.
Becomes a registered pharmacist.
Goes to Texas ranch with Dr. and Mrs. Hall; stays there two years.
Moves to Austin, Texas; lives as houseguest of Harrell family.
Becomes a cartographer in the Texas General Land Office; meets Athol Estes Roach, his future bride. They elope on July 1.
First child, a son, is born and dies shortly thereafter.
Daughter, Margaret Worth, is born on September 30; grandmother Ruth Worth Porter dies.
Loses position at the Land Office; gets job as teller at First National Bank of Austin.
First issue of *The Rolling Stone* appears on April 28; resigns from the bank in December.

Last issue of *The Rolling Stone* comes off the press on April 27; goes to work in the fall for the Houston *Post*.

Charged with embezzlement of bank funds; flees to Honduras to avoid his trial.

Returns to United States; turns himself in to face trial; Athol dies on July 25 at the age of twenty-nine.

Postponed trial begins on February 7; found guilty; enters Ohio State Penitentiary.

The first short story using the pen name O. Henry appears in December in *McClure's* magazine.

Released early from prison in July; goes to Pittsburgh to stay with the Roaches and Margaret.

Travels to New York City to become a writer, using pseudonym O. Henry.

Offered a contract by the *New York World* to write one story a week.

Marries Sara Coleman in Asheville, North Carolina.

Becomes ill and enters hospital on June 3; dies on June 5.

O. Henry Award Prize Stories competition begins.

Daughter Margaret Worth Porter Cesare Sartin dies in June at age thirty-eight.

Texas Heritage Foundation and Greensboro Writers Club unsuccessfully appeal to President Eisenhower for posthumous pardon for William Sydney Porter.

Russia issues memorial stamp; Greensboro Public Library observes centennial celebration of O. Henry's birth.

O. Henry Austin Museum named a national Literary Landmark.

Published Works

Cabbages and Kings, 1904
This novel is more of a loosely tied-together collection of short stories, consisting of many previously published stories and few that O. Henry added to hold the narrative together. It is composed of mostly Central American stories with a few of O. Henry's early New York stories.

The Four Million, 1906
In response to the statement that there were only 400 people worth knowing in New York City, O. Henry penned *The Four Million*. This collection centers on everyday people of the city—the poor, the homeless, the working girls and cab drivers. "The Gift of the Magi" belongs to this collection.

The Trimmed Lamp, 1907
The common people of New York City are again the heroes of *The Trimmed Lamp*. O. Henry creates a cast of deeply sympathetic characters that demand to be noticed. The unquestionable humanity of these lowly New Yorkers presents a stinging rebuke to those who reject them for their poverty and yet do nothing to relieve it.

Heart of the West, 1907
Heart of the West offers tales hailing mostly from the Texas range. Cisco Kid, the noble thief featured in "The Caballero's Way," has inspired many movies and television shows.

The Voice of the City, 1908
O. Henry returns to the East Coast to ruminate on both New Yorkers and the city itself. Does the city have a personality of its own? He sometimes uses other American cities to more clearly draw out the particular character of New York City.

The Gentle Grafter, 1908
Jeff Peters, the central character of *The Gentle Grafter*, is always cooking up a new plan to make money. He is a slick dresser and a level headed schemer, whose ideas nevertheless often go amusingly awry. O. Henry got his inspiration for shady Jeff from con stories told to him by fellow inmates while he was in the Ohio State Penitentiary.

Roads of Destiny, 1909
This collection has no unifying theme or character. The stories take place in Central America, Texas, New York and North Carolina. The title story, "Roads of Destiny," was made into a movie in 1921.

Options, 1909
A collection much like *Roads of Destiny,* this diverse group of stories continues to exhibit O. Henry's wit and his classic surprise endings.

Whirligigs, 1910
"The Ransom of Red Chief," which is probably O. Henry's best-known work, is found in this collection.

Strictly Business, 1910
Returning to the four million interesting people of New York, O. Henry gives one last concentrated look at the city.

Sixes and Sevens, 1911
One story in the collection, "The Last of the Troubadours," is thought to be among the best Western yarns ever told.

Rolling Stones, 1913
Most of these are early stories from O. Henry's days in Austin, Texas. The collection is named after the humorous magazine that he ran from 1894 to 1895, *The Rolling Stone.*

Waifs and Strays, 1917
Although many other anthologies of O. Henry's work have appeared over the years, this is the last collection of mostly unpublished work. Subsequent anthologies have simply reorganized the stories by theme or preference.

Letters:

Letter to Lithopolis, 1922
This book consists of several letters exchanged between O. Henry and Mabel Wagnalls.

Sources

CHAPTER ONE: Boyhood in the South

p. 12, "Oh, Henry . . ." Lollie Cave Wilson, *Hard to Forget: The Young O. Henry* (Los Angeles: Lyman House, 1939), 71.

p. 12-13, "I never met . . ." David Stuart, *O. Henry: A Biography of William Sydney Porter* (Chelsea, MI: Scarborough House Publishers, 1990), 139.

p. 14, "the best loved physician . . ." Eugene Current-Garcia, *O. Henry* (New Haven, CT: Twayne Publishers, Inc., 1965), 18.

p. 19, "I did more reading . . ." C. Alphonso Smith, *O. Henry* (New York: Chelsea House, 1980), 76.

p. 26, "the creepy sensation . . ." Gerald Langford, *Alias O. Henry: A Biography of William Sidney Porter.* (New York: The Macmillan Co., 1957), 13.

CHAPTER TWO: New Experiences

p. 27, "held a little court . . ." Langford, *Alias O. Henry*, 14.

p. 28, "Oh, that's Bill . . ." Robert H. Davis and Arthur B. Maurice, *The Caliph of Bagdad: O. Henry* (New York: D. Appleton and Company, 1931), 16.

p. 29, "I want you . . ." Richard O'Connor, *The Legendary Life of William S. Porter* (Garden City, NY: Doubleday and Company, 1970), 15.

p. 30, "Why don't you . . ." Wilson, *Hard to Forget*, 2.

p. 30, "What do girls . . ." Ibid.

p. 30-31, "Oh, I don't know . . ." Ibid., 6.

p. 31, "Southern girls . . ." Ibid., 2.

p. 34, "Forget that Porter . . ." Florence, Stratton, and Vincent Burke, *The White Plume* (Beaumont, TX: E. Szafir & Son Co., 1931), 24.

p. 35, "She has vamoosed . . ." Stuart, *O. Henry*, 37.

p. 35, "a young fellow here . . ." Langford, *Alias O. Henry*, 32.

p. 35, "I hesitated no longer . . ." Arthur W. Page, "Little Pictures of O. Henry; Part II—Texan Days," *The Bookman* 37 (July 1913), 500.

p. 36, "no sense of responsibility . . ." Langford, *Alias O. Henry*, 33.

p. 38, "the littlest man . . ." Page, "Texan Days," 502.

p. 41, "There was quite a time . . ." Ibid., 506.

CHAPTER THREE: Life in Austin

p. 42, "He learned bookkeeping . . ." Smith, *O. Henry*, 118.

p. 46, "The tableaux were all . . ." Frances Goggin Maltby, *The Dimity Sweetheart* (Richmond, VA: Press of the Dietz Printing Co., 1930), 20.

p. 46, "Look not back . . ." Ibid., 28.

p. 47, "I love you, Bill . . ." Wilson, *Hard to Forget*, 134.

p. 47, "Not sometime . . ." Ibid.

p. 47, "Honey, I am not . . ." Ibid., 133-134.

p. 47, "I'm going to be . . ." Maltby, *The Dimity Sweetheart*, 26.

p. 48, "Papa, it must be . . ." L. K. Smoot, personal letter (Austin History Center archives): 2.

p. 48, "There's romance . . ." Langford, *Alias O. Henry*, 51.

p. 48, "Oh, Will, my dress . . ." Ibid.

p. 48, "Marrying in a torn . . ." Wilson, *Hard to Forget*, 135.

p. 49, "God bless you . . ." Maltby, *The Dimity Sweetheart*, 32.

p. 49, "It will keep . . ." Ibid., 41.

p. 51, "I got off at . . ." O'Connor, *The Legendary Life of William S. Porter*, 38.

p. 54, "Porter, I took $300 . . ." Wilson, *Hard to Forget*, 139.

p. 56, "I just couldn't go . . ." Maltby, *The Dimity Sweetheart*, 49.

p. 56, "to know the joys . . ." Ibid., 53.

p. 58, "to fill its pages . . ." Current-Garcia, *O. Henry*, 70.

p. 58, "We would wander . . ." Edmunds Travis, "O. Henry's Austin Years," *Bunker's Monthly* 1:4 (April 1928), 507.

CHAPTER FOUR: Hard Times

p. 63, "It was a wonderful . . ." O. Henry, "Buried Treasure" in *The Complete Works of O. Henry* (Garden City, NY: Doubleday and Company, Inc., 1953), 1:738.

p. 67, "When I met him . . ." Langford, *Alias O. Henry*, 97.

p. 68, "I don't believe . . ." Al Jennings, *Through the Shadows with O. Henry* (New York: The H. K. Fly Company Publishers, 1921), 94.

p. 70, "Wire me twenty-five . . ." Langford, *Alias O. Henry*, 106.

p. 70, "she fairly radiated . . ." Ibid., 107.

p. 72, "Your story 'The Miracle . . ." O'Connor, *The Legendary Life of William S. Porter*, 64.

p. 72, "It might just as well . . ." Maltby, *The Dimity Sweetheart*, 77.

p. 73, "The money was gone . . ." Ruth Laughlin, "The Life of O. Henry: It Was His Best Story," *Greensboro Daily News*, 9 September 1962: C8.

p. 74, "I am absolutely . . ." Blanche Cotton Williams, *Our Short Story Writers* (Freeport, NY: Books for Libraries Press, 1969), 211.

CHAPTER FIVE: Prison and Redemption

p. 75, "I never stole . . ." Henry James Forman, "The Mystery of O. Henry," *Reader's Digest* (August 1947), 95.

p. 76, "I never imagined . . ." Smith, *O. Henry*, 155.

p. 77, "the diseased soul . . ." Jennings, *Through the Shadows*, 222.

p. 77, "I am busy . . ." Smith, *O. Henry*, 162.

p. 78, "July 8, 1898 . . ." Ibid., 158.

p. 78, "I'm so glad . . ." Ibid., 158-159.

p. 80, "May 17, 1900 . . ." Ibid., 161.

p. 80, "I hope your watch . . ." Ibid.

p. 80, "twenty nickels to spend . . ." Ibid.

p. 80-81, "October 1, 1900 . . ." Ibid., 161-162.

p. 81, "I'd have liked . . ." Ibid., 159-160.

p. 81, "I was . . . very, very . . ." Ibid., 161.

p. 81, "My dear Margaret . . ." Ibid., 165.

p. 81-82, "Now if you will . . ." Ibid., 161.

p. 82, "I am learning . . ." Ibid.

p. 82, "NO! He *never* told . . ." Howard Sartin, "Margaret and 'The Unknown Quantity.'" *Southern Humanities Review* 10 (Winter 1976): 11.

p. 82, "I have never . . ." O'Connor, *The Legendary Life of William S. Porter*, 66.

p. 85, "Hello, Bill . . ." Jennings, *Through the Shadows*, 298.

p. 87, "By the way, please . . ." Ibid., 264.

p. 87, "I thought he had . . ." Stuart, *O. Henry*, 130.

p. 88, "Writing is my business . . ." O'Connor, *The Legendary Life of William S. Porter*, 89.

p. 88-89, "When I first came . . ." Smith, *O. Henry*, 183.

CHAPTER SIX: Demand for Stories

p. 93, "There's something . . ." O. Henry, "The Chair of Philanthromathematics" in *The Complete Works of O. Henry* (Garden City, NY: Doubleday and Company, Inc., 1953), 1:285.

p. 94, "Gentlemen: I received your letter . . ." O. Henry, "The

Ransom of Red Chief" in *The Complete Works of O. Henry* (Garden City, NY: Doubleday and Company, Inc., 1953), 2:1151.

p. 94, "something vital, warm . . ." O'Connor, *The Legendary Life of William S. Porter*, 189.

p. 96, "became a prison . . ." Langford, *Alias O. Henry*, 183.

p. 96, "He shrank from . . ." O'Connor, *The Legendary Life of William S. Porter*, 101.

p. 97, "Just make sure . . ." Ibid., 106.

p. 98, "Since you have been . . ." William Sydney Porter, *Letters to Lithopolis from O. Henry to Maria Wagnalls*, 2d ed. (Austin, TX: Eakin Press, 1999), 2.

p. 98, "I would like to live . . ." Smith, *O. Henry*, 233.

p. 98-99, "No one who has . . ." Porter, *Letters to Lithopolis*, xxiii-xxiv.

p. 99, "Then suddenly, as he . . ." O. Henry, "The Furnished Room" in *The Complete Works of O. Henry* (Garden City, NY: Doubleday and Company, Inc., 1953), 1:101.

p. 100, "Across the counter . . ." O'Connor, *The Legendary Life of William S. Porter*, 125.

p. 100, "All the reforms . . ." Maria M. Connolly, "The Letters of O. Henry—Look Between the Lines," *Greensboro Daily News*, 9 September 1962, C9.

p. 100-101, "Dulcie worked in . . ." O. Henry, "An Unfinished Story" in *The Complete Works of O. Henry* (Garden City, NY: Doubleday and Company, Inc., 1953), 1:72-74.

p. 103, "My book will bring . . ." O'Connor, *The Legendary Life of William S. Porter,* 139.

p. 104, "A favorite dodge . . ." Eugene Current-Garcia, *O. Henry: A Study of the Short Fiction* (New York: Twayne Publishers, 1993), 52.

p. 105, "The mountains reached . . ." O. Henry, "Smith" in *Complete Works of O. Henry* (Garden City, NY: Doubleday,

1953), 1:574.

p. 105, "The author, who has . . ." Stuart, *O. Henry*, 157.

p. 105, "With his stories . . ." Langford, *Alias O. Henry*, 194-195.

p. 106, "Here's a dollar . . ." Smith, *O. Henry*, 168.

p. 107, "I don't want to . . ." Ibid.

p. 107, "Don't you think . . ." Ibid.

p. 107-108, "You can't write . . ." E. Hudson Long, *O. Henry: The Man and His Work* (New York: A. S. Barnes and Company, Inc., 1949), 129.

CHAPTER SEVEN: Second Marriage

p. 109-110, "My dear 'Miss Sally' . . ." Connolly, "The Letters of O. Henry," C9.

p. 111, "Not very long ago . . ." Long, *O. Henry*, 124-125.

p. 112, "I'll tell you what . . ." O'Connor, *The Legendary Life of William S. Porter*, 158.

p. 112, "Lie down there . . ." Forman, "The Mystery of O. Henry," 92.

p. 114, "The reader who skips . . ." Stuart, *O. Henry*, 212.

p. 117, "They sped upon velvety . . ." O. Henry, "Hygeia at the Solito" in *The Complete Works of O. Henry* (Garden City, NY: Doubleday and Company, Inc., 1953), 1:157.

p. 118-119, "Mr. Porter's new volume . . ." Langford, *Alias O. Henry*, 212.

p. 119, "A new book of stories . . ." Ibid., 218.

p. 120, "His creations are so . . ." Ibid., 223.

p. 120, "I'm a failure . . ." Ibid., 224.

p. 120, "I want to show . . ." Current-Garcia, *O. Henry: A Study*, 159.

p. 121, "A play is something . . ." Seth Moyle, *My Friend O. Henry* (New York: The H. K. Fly Company Publishers, 1914), 19.

p. 121, "Not at all . . ." Forman, "The Mystery of O. Henry," 95-96.

p. 123, "I want to get . . ." Smith, *O. Henry*, 248.

p. 123, "I could look . . ." Ibid., 173.

p. 123, "darker angel" Langford, *Alias O. Henry*, 236.

p. 123, "full of good stories . . ." Stuart, *O. Henry*, 220.

p. 124, "I'm back in New York . . ." O'Connor, *The Legendary Life of William S. Porter*, 224.

p. 124, "encyclopaedic account . . ." Langford, *Alias O. Henry*, 242.

p. 125, "I'm sick, Anne . . ." Dale Kramer, *The Heart of O. Henry* (New York: Rinehart & Company, Inc., 1954), 305.

p. 127, "Turn up the lights . . ." Smith, *O. Henry*, 250.

CHAPTER EIGHT: An Enigma

p. 129, "His [O. Henry's] style . . ." O'Connor, *The Legendary Life of William S. Porter*, 235.

p. 135, "was never that of . . ." Ibid., 120.

p. 135, "God sent him . . ." Sartin, "Margaret and 'The Unknown Quantity,'" 2.

p. 135, "And now we will . . ." "O. Henry's Daughter Weds on Death Bed," n.p.

p. 137, "O. Henry did not . . ." Joyce Kilmer, "Is O. Henry a Pernicious Literary Influence?" *New York Times Magazine* (23 June 1916): 12.

p. 137, "Let's have another . . ." Current-Garcia, *O. Henry*, 158.

p. 137, "the whole English . . ." Ibid.

p. 138, "In the whole canon . . ." O'Connor, *The Legendary Life of William S. Porter*, 236.

p. 139, "To condemn O. Henry's . . ." Current-Garcia, *O. Henry*, 237.

Bibliography

Connolly, Marie M. "The Letters of O. Henry—Look Between the Lines." *Greensboro Daily News,* 9 September 1962, 1, 9 (C).

Current-Garcia, Eugene. *O. Henry (William Sydney Porter).* New York: Twayne Publishers, Inc., 1965.

———. *O. Henry: A Study of the Short Fiction.* New York: Twayne Publishers, 1993.

Davis, Robert H., and Arthur B. Maurice. *The Caliph of Bagdad: O. Henry.* D. Appleton and Company, 1931.

Forman, Henry James. "The Mystery of O. Henry," *Reader's Digest,* August 1947, 92-96.

Harris, Richard C. *William Sidney Porter (O. Henry): A Reference Guide.* Boston: G. K. Hall & Co., 1980.

Henry, O. *The Complete Works of O. Henry.* 2 vols. Garden City, NY: Doubleday and Company, Inc., 1953.

Jennings, Al. *Through the Shadows with O. Henry.* New York: The H. K. Fly Company, 1921.

Kilmer, Joyce. "Is O. Henry a Pernicious Literary Influence?" *New York Times Magazine,* 23 January 1916, 12.

Kramer, Dale. *The Heart of O. Henry*. New York: Rinehart & Company, Inc., 1954.

Langford, Gerald. *Alias O. Henry: A Biography of William Sidney Porter*. New York: The Macmillan Co., 1957.

Laughlin, Ruth. "O. Henry: His Life Was His Best Story," *Greensboro Daily News*, 9 September 1962, 8 (C).

Long, E. Hudson. *O. Henry: The Man and His Work*. New York: A. S. Barnes and Company, Inc., 1949.

Maltby, Frances Goggin. *The Dimity Sweetheart*. Richmond, VA: Press of The Dietz Printing Co., 1930.

Moyle, Seth. *My Friend O. Henry*. New York: The H. K. Fly Company, 1914.

O'Connor, Richard. *O. Henry: The Legendary Life of William S. Porter*. Garden City, New York: Doubleday and Company, Inc. 1970.

"O. Henry's Daughter Weds on Death Bed." *Houston Press*, 23 June 1927: n.p.

Page, Arthur W. "Little Pictures of O. Henry; Part II—Texan Days," *The Bookman* 37, no. 5 (July 1913): 498-508.

Porter, William Sydney, *Letters to Lithopolis from O. Henry to Maria Wagnalls,* 2d ed. Austin, TX: Eakin Press, 1999.

Sartin, Howard. "Margaret and 'The Unknown Quantity.'" *Southern Humanities Review*, 10, no. 1 (Winter 1976): 1-18.

Smith, C. Alphonso. *O. Henry Biography*. New York: Doubleday, Page and Company, 1916.

Smoot, L. K. Original letter of remembrances (Austin History Center archives).

Stratton, Florence, and Vincent Burke. *The White Plume*. Beaumont, TX: E. Szafir & Son Co., 1931.

Stuart, David. *O. Henry: A Biography of William Sydney Porter*. Chelsea, MI: Scarborough House Publishers, 1990.

Travis, Edmunds. "O. Henry's Austin Years: An Account of the Life of William Sydney Porter in the Capital City of Texas."

Bunker's Monthly 1, no. 4 (April 1918): 486-508.

Williams, Blanche Cotton. *Our Short Story Writers*. Freeport, NY: Books for Libraries Press, 1969.

Wilson, Lollie Cave. *Hard to Forget: The Young O. Henry*. Los Angeles: Lyman House, 1939.

Web sites

www.greensborohistory.org/
The Greensboro Historical Museum Web site provides information on collections, tours, and archives, including a link to information about the O. Henry exhibit.

www.ci.austin.tx.us/parks/ohenry.htm
The restored home of William Sidney Porter contains artifacts and memorabilia from Porter's life in Austin. Web site includes a photo gallery.

www.gutenberg.org
An online collection of over seventeen thousand free e-books that are in the public domain. The site offers the complete text of more than a dozen O. Henry stories.

www.randomhouse.com/anchor/ohenry/
The official site of the O. Henry Prize.

Index